BEEBUZZARDS ATOP THE CARCASS

Clarence W. Dawson

SUNSTONE
PRESS

To
Clark L. Loomis,
my very estimable buddy
with whom I have shared
a priceless friendship.

First Edition

Printed in the United States of America

Library of Congress Cataloging in Publication Data
Dawson, Clarence W., 1915-
    Beebuzzards atop the carcass / Clarence W. Dawson.—1st ed.
        p.   cm.
    ISBN 0-86534-174-5 : $14.95
    1. Dawson, Clarence W.,1915-   —Childhood and youth. I. Title.
    CT275.D3116A3   1993
    306.874'2'092—dc20   92-22026
    [B]   CIP

Published by   SUNSTONE PRESS
                      Post Office 2321
                      Santa Fe, NM 87504-2321 / USA

CONTENTS

CHAPTER ONE

Rogues or Saints?

Had our mothers seen Carl and me send those stimulating volts into a pair of wired tacks on the outhouse oval upon which sluggish-entrailed Cousin Boyd was roosting, they probably would have contended defendingly: "They're not really mean, you know — just mischievous." Well, the dears might have been right, and then again...but you be the jury.

Let me insist from the outset, however, that paradoxical as my comment may appear, we did seem to entertain certain principles of nobility even from the time when we first formed our "mischievous" two-membered fraternity, The Royal Society of the Beebuzzards.

There was the time, for instance, when we threw a switch during the evening church service, placed a huge collie on the pew beside Mr. Loyd McKinney, and then turned on the lights again to let the members of the congregation see that shaggy beast slobbering contentedly beside his bewildered neighbor.

How respectful of us to postpone darkening the santuary until the minister had called for the offering and Cousin Boyd had dropped his finger into a collection plate to jostle the coins into rattling an impression that he had made a contribution! We waited, in fact, until the conclusion of the following prayer, until the choir began to howl a classical which we were positive no one except the musicians themselves and that dog could appreciate. Our little prank, then, was really but an intermission lodged between the scripture reading and the sermon coming up.

Then there was the occasion of the college sophomore picnic when we poured croton oil, a fluid drive much more potent than its relative castor, into a bowl of potato salad. Again we proved that we were not without scruples, for we were careful to place the persuasive drops in food which Professor Holdbolt would not eat, for we knew that the man must have had a good reason for nestling so often on that inflated cushion he always carried to class and to the bleachers.

Nor can you ignore the nuptial affair when we hid in a community house closet, poked an air rifle through the partially ajar door and peppered the bald crest of the best man as he Saint Vitus danced down the aisle. Once again our keen sense of kindliness and consideration for others forbade our popping the shiny target except during those moments when the organ was playing. We did not want the sound of falling shot to detract from the sacredness of the marriage vows. How could we have been more considerate?

And what about the time we leaned over the rail of a theater balcony to dump that glass of angry ants into the lonely lap of Miss Presley, a spinster of many moons standing? What other youths would have been kind enough to wait until the lady had seen half of the double-feature? In a way we were really sweet to drop the insects, for had Miss Presley remained to see the ensuing show she would have been saddened. You see, it was a love picture, and our subject was a faded refugee from Beautyland, a forlorn maid whose grape of hope had long ago withered to raisinhood.

Why do you shake your head? Do you really believe we were mean?

Well, I can take a hint. I understand now how you feel about us. And I was hoping you wouldn't be prejudiced.

Possibly you are wondering what we finally became in adult life. Then hang around with us in these pages to follow and we'll try to satisfy your curiosity.

Are you really sure that we came to naught but ill? Now suppose Carl were to invite you to come hear him in the pulpit, or suppose I asked you to attend my series of lectures on the Beatitudes? Now wouldn't you feel ashamed for having so hastily condemned us just because of a few little boyish pranks that perpetually insisted on imposing themselves upon us?

On the other hand, it may be that you'll want to keep reading with the passionate hope you'll learn our prison address so that you can walk past our quarters sometime and toss a hand grenade our way.

CHAPTER TWO

Heckling the Bowlegged Redhead

Soft music and a pageant of everchanging spotlight colors surrounded by darkness accompanied a slightly bowlegged beauty
contestant as she turned her redheaded features to a Rex Theater
audience and promenaded in her scanty attire across the stage.

Just as she was twisting her strawberry contours midway across
the runway, the girl stopped, startled by a youthful voice from the
balcony.

"Oh, my gosh?" it screamed. "Take it away! I can't stand the
sight!"

"Be quiet, Carl!" I urged in a whisper. "One more crack like that
and that usher'll throw us out sure."

We snickered and watched the redhead try to fan away her
humiliation by throwing her middle into several fast curves that
started out to be seductive but soon fell amateurishly by the wayside.

You will possibly laugh me to scorn when I explain the why of my
companion's depreciating outburst. In spite of what you may think,
we Beebuzzards were, after a fashion, old-fashioned, and in Carl's
subconscious thinking it was not proper that fire-haired Betsy Snerd,
a Christian Epworth League worker scheduled for wedding knots two
days hence, should so parade her unveiled torso in invitation to this
racy applause.

A brigade of renewed whistling was just beginning to hearld the
appearance of another contestant when a taut finger stabbed me in
my shoulder blade.

A form bent over me and became audible with: "The manager
don't like for anybody to say things like you did a minute ago. Please
don't do that again."

It was an usher — the crossed-eyed one, or "the strabismus," as
we called Atkins.

"Which one of us are you looking at, fella?" Carl inquired,
scrutinizing the man's crossed orbs.

Quite evidently offended, Atkins pulled his finger out of my shoulder, apparently aimed it at my nose and replied, "This guy right here!"

"Aw, come on now," protested Carl, "he didn't say a thing...not a thing! If you're referring to that little harmless comment that was made when the redhead came out, I can give you my word of honor Nelson didn't do it."

"Well, one of you guys did."

"What proof do you have, Strabismus?" Carl did not feel himself mean in using that big word to address Atkins, for he knew the latter did not know it meant *cross-eyed.*

"Well, that remark came from somewhere right up here, and...."

The theater vibrated again as a vivacious blonde brought forth a volley of applause in which Carl and I participated.

"Strabismus," said Carl, when the noise had gone with the blonde, "do you mean that without tangible evidence to substantiate your contention you have the audacity to charge us two spectators with having been offensive by hurling obnoxious invectives?"

Carl and I, English majors in junior and sophomore years respectively, were serious students of diction, a subject we studied independently as well as in college. We were secretly proud of the fact that a few of the local high school girls termed us the "Walking Dictionaries," and we were sometimes addicted to parading our vocabularies, particularly before a dullard like this usher.

When Atkins finished gaping his blank confusion he pulled in his teeth and said as if he were pleading for us to confess our guilt, "Well, heck, fellas, them calls came from over here, and, heck, everybody in town knows you guys are...sort of...."

"Now stop right there, Atkins!" Carl demanded as he elevated his five feet ten inches to the chin of the heavier and taller man confronting him.

"Down in front, please!" someone requested a few rows behind.

"Come on outside, Atkins," Carl challenged.

"I didn't call you anything, Lewis," the usher hurried to say as we moved toward the stairway. By now he had probably remembered my buddy's nickname — "Sharkey," an appellation Carl had acquired because his boxing ability was not unlike that of Sharkey the professional heavyweight.

"No, but you were on the point of doing it," I contributed, feeling I ought not to remain completely out of developments.

In the velvety lobby, my welterweight partner, who had been leading the way, stopped, faced Atkins and let his blue eyes blaze indignantly. "Now, Strabismus," he said, "we're a coupla good peaceable lads who don't like trouble, see? But if it's necessary, we're always prepared to defend ourselves and our honor."

"Well, I haven't done nothing."

"I beg your pardon, Strabismus, but you have," Carl contradicted. "You have brought an accusation against us that we just don't like. See?"

"Well, heck, fellas, I'm sorry if I made you mad."

Carl sipped a breath through his symmetrical teeth and let his eyes soften to a tone of triumph.

"It's okay this time," he conceded. "Just don't let it happen again."

Since the beauty parade was now over, I suggested to my companion that we "go get something to drink."

Just as we stepped out on the sidewalk, a green apple whizzed close over my head.

"Nab the little devil!" exclaimed Carl as we streaked in pursuit of the Latin-American bootblack who had thrown at us.

Breathless as a pair of Peeping Toms en route to a nudist colony, we gave up the chase several blocks away and turned into a nearby drugstore for our contemplated refreshments.

"Squirt us a pair of cherry phosphates," I requested of an adolescent soda jerk who apparently was trying to decide whether he wanted to eat the nut sundae before him or go all out on a pimple-picking project.

"You guys been taking some roadwork?" the beaver-toothed boy wanted to know.

"Nope, just been playing tag with a street urchin," replied Carl, looking with gustatory anticipation at the drink.

"Ketch'im?"

"Nope."

"Those kids sure do hate you guys. That was the funniest thing I ever did see when Sharkey put his hand against Ernesto Lozano's stomick and flipped him over so fast Ernesto didn't know what was comin' off. You ever see him do it, Lefty?"

"Certainly, Al," I answered. "Do you think I could hang around Sharkey all this time without seeing his famous bootblack wheel in action?"

"Is that what you call it? Say, Shark, how 'bout teaching me how to do that? I'll make these drinks free and fill 'em up again, if you will. It won't hurt me, will it?"

The pair of straws through which Carl had just begun to suck the phosphate became white again long enough for him to reply: "Nope, it doesn't hurt anybody...just scares a laundry job out of these shoeshine boys, though."

His erectile mustache of auburn spines making whoopee on his flabby upper lip, fair-faced Bernard Snerd, brother of the girl my companion had heckled on the stage, stepped up at this moment to the fountain and interposed his well-groomed and slightly delicate self between Carl and me, whom he graced with an almost formal "Hello, Nelson and Lewis."

We had hardly returned the newcomer's greeting when Carl winked a signal to me which I readily understood to suggest that we engage in one of our conversational abracadabras for the benefit of our acquaintance, one who always seemed to hold himself aloof from us and all we represented...or perhaps misrepresented.

Seeming to ignore our "victim," I rattled the ice in my glass, looked at Lewis and said: "So you're really going to buy that shotgun?"

"No," replied the addressee, "I think I'll just roast a duck instead."

"But, Carl, you can't do that...not if the radishes bloom in December."

"The heck I can't! Didn't you ever hear of a Tweed's selling for 35 dollars, after a rain in the pines?"

"Certainly, but the light in the widow's window was green until the frog croaked bird shot."

If we had not been so apparently serious and had Snerd been unaware of the cool social gulf that had ever stood between him and us, he might have let his noggin put on a windshield wiper act and he might have laughed. But respecting circumstances, he merely cut his eyes back and forth without turning his head, pretending ever so hard to give the impression he hadn't heard our flow of nonsense. Perhaps it was that vain pretension which amused us so much.

"Well," I said, resuming our talk, "I once read a book that milked a cow at dawn while a cricket serenaded a garter factory."

"But, Lawrence, you can't smell smoke till the sun sets in China behind a willow stump."

"That's exactly what I told my Aunt Susie. I said, 'Man, you can't ride a bicycle standing up backwards and smoking a cigar.' "

Al cackled in amusement, Snerd nonchantly crunched some ice pebbles, and Carl maintained a sober countenance only by biting his lips and pinching his leg. As for me, I blew my nose to cover up my merriment. Only sheer will power which we had developed for use on occasions like this enabled us to restrain our yearning to join Al in his loud laughter.

Finally, after an awkward silence, Snerd slapped a quarter on the counter, picked up his change, and without glancing at either of us Beebuzzards, strutted away through the doorway to the sidewalk outside, little dreaming of the sad hand the Beebuzzards were to deal him at a later date.

Three sets of guffaws sprayed the drugstore with vociferous vibration. It was the most Carl and I had laughed since we beheld in a filling station rest room a neatly printed placard appealing, "PLEASE DO NOT LEAVE THIS STOOL WHILE BOWELS ARE IN MOTION."

CHAPTER THREE

Candidate for the "Pore Houses"

It was another night and Carl and I were on our way to buy our favorite ambrosia, watermelon. From behind a shadowy mountain some 15 miles eastward, the crown of a punctured moon peered over Old Rusty, a snaggle-toothed peak of solid rock, and silhouetted the rustic features of a Mexican store 100 yards forward.

"If we can't get a melon there, we'll just be out of luck," Carl commented, picking up a mesquite root and hurling it at a challenging bulldog, who stood tiptoeing his ugly features over a wire fence.

"Well, if the man doesn't have a good one, let's just substitute a half gallon of ice cream," I replied above the yelps bounding back from the root-receiving canine.

Sheltered by a rusty metallic shade, a dim light over the adobe store building sucked in bugs from the air and illuminated a windworn sign that advertised: MARTINEZ GROCERY.

Whenever the opportunity presented itself, we were prone to inoculate the most commonplace with some spicy bit of foolishness. Right now the opportunity was presenting itself.

Bells tinkling on the screen door announced us to the blubbery proprietor, a short man of 200 pounds bundled in a white apron.

"Mr. Martinez?" inquired Carl, extending his hand to vibrate the heavy human bulk before him.

"Sí, Sí. That's how I call myself."

"Then, Mr. Martinez, let me introduce myself. I'm Thomas Jefferson, and this is Mr. Alexander Hamilton."

Well, what did this simple man know about United States history?

"I'm glad to meet you, Meester Jeff and Meester Alexhandgo. I can do something for you?"

With stiff formality and stilted diction, Carl answered: "It is quite possible you may be of service to us, Mr. Martinez."

"Mr. Martinez," I added, "The Royal Order of the Beebuzzards will be most grateful, if you can be of help."

"Martinez always try to please all the world, Meester Alexhandgo."

"Precisely why we are here, Behemoth." Wasn't it all right for Carl to call the proprietor "Behemoth" so long as the latter didn't know the word is used in Job to describe an animal which was probably the hippopotamus?

"You see," he continued, after much deliberation, "we Beebuzzards have elected your store to be our official supply post. Needless to say, you are to be commended and felicitated. Mr. Martinez, permit me to congratulate you!"

Carl grasped his left hand and I took his right and we squeezed with all our might until the congratulated one jerked his pinched fingers loose and said, "You fellows, you have soam smokes."

"Thanks, but we don't smoke," I declined.

"Mr. Martinez, we have descended upon your humble establishment tonight for the purpose of effecting a purchase."

"Wot you say, Meester Jeff?"

"I say we want to buy a good melon. You got one?" Carl's sudden discontinuation of his formal speech pattern evidently indicated that he was becoming eager to eat watermelon.

We trailed behind the waddling one as he led us through pyramids of canned goods and hills of bulging sacks.

"You like thees?" he asked. He punctuated his sentence with a slap at a mosquito which had determined to drill for blood in the crest of the man's hatless head.

"We're used to good melons, Mr. Martinez," I informed him. "If we can't get a good melon, we don't want any."

"These melon all gude."

"You guarantee they're good?"

"If these melons no gude, I make them gude."

"I beg your pardon, sir," contested Sharkey with a return to bombast, "but these melons are either good or they are not. Nature makes them inferior, mediocre, or superior. And you are not endowed with some fantastic power which enables you to change their quality."

"Wot, Meester, Jeff?"

"I said you can't change a bad melon into a good melon."

"No, Meester Jeff, I cannot do thees. But you meesunderstand. I say if a melon no gude you don't pay."

"Then my advice to you is simply: `In promulgating your esoteric cogitations, or articulating your superficial sentimentalities and amicable, philosophical, or psychological observations, beware of platitudinous ponderosity. Let your conversations and communications possess a clarified conciseness....' "

"Meester Jeff!" the Latin stormed, explosively interrupting a quotation Carl had memorized. "I don' know wot you say to me!" This time his heavy hand fell more impatiently than ever on his sleek head and again the mosquito whined away untouched.

They were piled in a green heap — long striped melons whose round ends peeked at us as though somehow inviting us to thump their smooth bellies.

"How much is this berry?" I asked, singling out one of the very largest and examining its stem.

"That one I geeve you for 25 cents."

"Twenty-five cents!" we ejaculated in unison, pretending to be outraged.

"Mr. Martinez." After addressing the storekeeper, Carl drew in a jawful of air and let it skim out through his teeth bared by half-curled lips. And then melodramatically he unleased: "It's men like you who make the world unsafe for the establishment of democracy. Shall we go back to our Beebuzzard Society and inform the huge membership that they have made a mistake in electing you their official supply agent? Shall we inform them that their choice is, in reality, a mercenary capitalist whose consuming greed exceeds his sense of honor, that...."

"Okay, okay! I make the price 20 cents!" Even if Martinez had been able to fully comprehend Carl's charge, he might not have been troubled by what "the huge membership" would think of him, but he *was* troubled by that confounding flow of words and it was worth a nickel to him to stop it.

Whipping out a long pocketknife, the storekeeper suggested interrogatively, "You want that I plug eet?"

"Cut it all the way through," I instructed. "We want to see the heart."

"Yes," agreed Carl. "Stab its jugular vein and let it bleed. Yea, even unto the death! Let fall the blade, knave!"

"Jeff, you are a merciless fiend," I said, sharing my buddy's tone of Shakespearean melodramatics. "Alas, that you should speak with this brutal barbarism."

For a moment the fat man looking hesitantly at the two of us plainly showed his shaken confidence in our sanity.

"All right!" barked Sharkey. "Get the lead out! Rush it up. Don't just stand there like a jackass on an iceberg!"

"Sí, sí!" Martinez responded. His rolling beef straddled the melon, he bent low and then with undulating grunts he hacked until the melon lay apart.

"Too ripe," pronounced Carl.

"Okay, you peek another. We cut eet."

We selected another melon, pushed the price down a nickel, and shoved it to the Behemoth.

"Too stringly and tough," I condemned when the red meat was open to view.

"You taste eet. If she don' taste gude, you don' pay."

"You dern right we don't pay!" said Carl as he reached down and detached the core of one of the halves.

Martinez watched hopefully while we devoured the juicy heart, but his hopes were short-lived. Carl's forehead ridged in support of my contention.

"You don' like?"

"Nope." Sharkey rolled out another melon.

Again the grunts. Again the red meat lay bare.

"¡Qué bueno!" exclaimed the grocer.

"Bueno the devil!" snorted my companion. "I wouldn't let a vulture eat that thing, much less a beebuzzard."

"Then I don' got the melon for you. We cannot make the trade."

Martinez panted to his feet, looked sadly over the array of crimson waste and said: "I get to the pore houses queek thees way. Gude-buye, Meester Jeff. Gude-buye, Meester Alexhandgo. Maybe someday you find wot you look for."

He had turned his back and was shaking his massive weight away from us when Sharkey took hold of the man's apron and said above the rip of cheesecloth: "Now just one moment, Martinez."

I don't know whether or not the bulky one meant to branish the long pocketknife as a weapon. At any rate, when he turned with it and a menacing face which at last showed anger, we suddenly concluded that violence was really an undesirable thing.

"Mr. Martinez, we're sorry," I hastened to say, "that we've put you to all this trouble."

"Eet is not but the trouble. Just luke at all thees juicy, gude melon gone to waste!"

"Well, let's have one more try at it, Mart," proposed Carl. "If this next one isn't...."

"No, by gollys! You don' know the gude melon. You just want to cut and cut till all the melon gone! Then you go out and tell at the people: `We cut all Martinez' melon till hees store luke like the stuck hog factory. Then all the world sneeker and slobber at Martinez and geeve heem the haw haw."

"Martinez," Carl blew through his teeth, "do you know Attorney Donald Jeter?"

"The lawyer man?"

"Yes,"

"Si, I know heem."

"Well, he's my uncle," lied Carl. "And knowing that I am preparing myself to be a lawyer, Uncle Donald has been teaching me the laws and regulations governing our little city of Mesa. Naturally then, Behemoth, I am acquainted with Article X, Section 3 of the city constitution. Now then, I ask you: what do you intend to do about Article X, Section 3?"

"Arteecle wot?"

"Is it possible you are not acquainted with Article X, Section 3 which states that, whereas, party of the first part having begun a business transaction with the party of the second part, and, whereas, party of the second part has encouraged party of the first part to purchase a commodity, party of the second part shall not deny party of the first part the privilege of terminating the purchase?"

"I don' go to school much, Meester Jeff. Tell me some other way wot you try to say to me."

"Just this: If a man starts a trade with a customer he's got to finish it. Comprende?"

"Si, si, yo comprendo, ahora."

Our grocer missed the mosquito again but blotched his head.

"Okay, okay!" he said after a moment of muddled deliberation. "I don' know nothing about thees arteecle, so I'm gonna geeve you the benefit. But, by George, I'm gonna also tell thees to your huncle and see eef you geeve to me the cheat."

Four cuttings later, I handed the forlorn man 15 cents, we each took half a melon in hand and made a hopscotch exit through a hog's version of red and green heaven cluttering up the floor.

Beyond the earshot of the store we paused to release ourselves in a spasm of laughter. We laughed about as much as we did one morning when we sprinkled high life on the rump of a donkey whose bridle rein caught the leg of his unseated rider and caused the unhappy man to curse shamelessly when his blustering animal dragged him across a cactus plant.

CHAPTER FOUR

Salting Down the Janitor

Had we been conventional, we might have been entangled that night in the arms of a couple of sweet-smelling coeds and necking musically on waxed floors to the blare of the local collegiate orchestra. But being unconventional youths, we preferred tonight to "break" into the church — our church in which we were two were members of a Methodist youth group called the Epworth League.

And so tonight we would steal clandestinely into the basement of the aged yellow building and there finish writing a satire about two haughty, toe-headed girls who had rudely rejected the friendship we offered. Since the editor of the college paper was our friend, we hoped the pair would see printed in the weekly *Tatler* our sarcastic poem which, of course, would be anonymous.

With a few Hawaiian twists, Sharkey's dilapidated Model T coupe, which we Beebuzzards called "The Carcass," shimmied to a standstill and coughed fitfully a rooster crow from a street light which showed the gabled outline of our destination.

"You have the dictionary, I guess," said I.

"Right here," my buddy responded, patting Webster's brainchild.

The rusty doors of The Carcass rasped complainingly, we stepped out into the crisp October air, crossed a canal of liquid adobe, and vigilantly walked to the rear of the ecclesiastical edifice.

Scarcely aided by the illumination from the street, we punched a wire through a screen, raised a window we had unlocked Sunday night after the evening service, and slipped down into a basement room where on Sabbaths our class was accustomed to meet.

"Hope that confounded sheriff won't visit us again tonight." Sharkey remembered the time a neighboring resident who had been requested to watch for two "prowlers" had summoned an officer. We had barely eluded him.

Since that time, however, we had discovered our "rat hole," a nook whose floor was dirt and whose ceiling was partly a conglomeration of gas and water pipes. It was an inhuman place, even for a Beebuzzard, but it afforded us rather safe refuge in time of need.

After drawing each shade and switching on a light, we built a fire in the stove at the southern end of the classroom.

"You know if we weren't such refined lads," remarked Sharkey as he mangled a stick of licorice, "we'd probably torn up a chair for this fire, instead of fetching wood from the furnace room."

The blonde sisters who had incurred our ill will and who were to be the subjects of our writing were members of our Sunday School class and were fellow students—sophomores at our college. Their sole distinction, so far as we could see, lay...well, let our satire tell you about it.

We worked laboriously for two hours.

"Here's mine," said Carl finally, thrusting out his suggestion for the concluding line in our collaboration.

Two or three minutes later, I handed him my contribution, and then using the two tentative verses we worked orally together until we constructed a final line which met the satisfaction of us both.

"Gentlemen," said Carl, rising dramatically and addressing an imaginary host of 40,000 mythical pledges of the Beebuzzard Society, "we give you 'The Campus Flirts'."

"Will the members please rise and remain standing during the sacred reading?" I requested of the non-existing company.

Pretending to wait until the 40,000 had lumbered to their feet, my collaborator then let his face fall into a comfortable sneer and read:

> " 'With chatter, chatter, here they come,
> With swinging hips and chewing gum;
> And from their lofty perch on high,
> They slight the lowly passerby.
> They flitter by with flaunting grace,
> With tilted nose and painted face,
> Flamboyant lips and crimson cheek,
> With massive and protruding beak.' "

Here Carl paused to let the 40,000 cheer before continuing with:

> " 'A pair of fickle, frivolous flirts, whose
>   smug, complacent air
> Betrays their selfish self esteem and does
>   a pride declare.
> On Sunday morn they come to church bedecked
>   in rich array;
>
> They seize two seats but not to hear what
>   teacher has to say,

But rather that their floppy hats may all
    the crowd impress,
That all the lowly common folk may learn
    how "ladies" dress.
Their cheeks now decked with excess rouge
    to hide each sallow crack,
Their hair is sprayed with cheap perfume,
    their eyelids draped in black.
The day of aviation this, let hips fly
    where they may.
The greater range the wider swath, the
    more appeal they say'."

Again the pause, again the bow, again the settling sneer. Carl, co-president of the Royal Society of the Beebuzzards, read the last stanza:

" `And yet one thing we two will say;
Indeed a compliment we'll pay.
In spite of all the verdant hounds
Who prowl around the campus grounds
And oftentimes in gangs abound
In groups where toe-heads two are found,
We do admire the noisy pop
When chewing gum their jaws they flop'."

"I give you a toast, gentlemen," said I, holding aloft an ebony stick of licorice.

Sharkey cornered a similar stick in his own pocket and followed suit.

I was about to propose the toast when he gestured for silence.

"Somebody's outside!" he whispered.

"How do you know?"

"Didn't you hear that shuffling in the...."

I heard it this time: — the sound of crunching cottonwood leaves near the window through which we had gained admittance.

"Quick, douse the lights!" was Carl's excited urgency.

Voicing eerie creaks and squeaks, the floor protested our groping across its dry surface.

"Let's look through this one." My fellow fugitive turned up a near-by shade an inch or two so that we might scrutinize our visitor.

The old chap stood there pointing the rays of his flashlight at the screen with the punched hole. It was the janitor.

A car attempting to turn around in front of the building had momentarily spotlighted him, revealing his meager figure enveloped in black corduroy trousers and a brown gabardine jacket, his long-billed cap that ran a close race with his hooked nose and yet failed to conceal his bulging eyes, and his shaggy hair protruding unashamed from a pair of droopy ears.

His name was McKinney, but, to his face, Carl called him "Mr. McPenny" and I called him "Mr. McSkinny." Because somehow he had outwitted us in several of our attempts to ensnare him in some mischievous trap, we also referred to him as "Foxy Mack."

"Say, guy, I've got an idea!" The ring in Carl's voice told me that we were not going to take the defensive tonight and withdraw to the rat hole.

Without stopping to explain his plan, my buddy led our dark journey to the kitchen. There we shut the door and turned on the lights.

"Be looking for some salt," said Carl. He was placing a big dish pan under a running faucet in the sink.

By the time the pan was full, I had located a package of salt. We dissolved it all in the water and were about to leave when Carl stopped, put the pan down and said, "Wait a minute. I just thought of something else we might add."

We emptied a pint of vinegar in the salt solution and were hurrying with it down a hallway to the classroom when I saw Foxy Mack's flashlight beam moving along the ground like a sniffling bloodhound toward the front entrance.

"Upstairs with it!" I instructed.

By the time the poking janitor had reached his destination, we were perched in a window of the second story overlooking his lowly position opposite the door which he intended to unlock.

Suddenly my partner aimed a murderous yell at the victim. With a vibrant start that shook his cap down farther on his knobby head, the latter tossed his chin skyward and was about to bathe us with his light when Carl drenched him with the salt and vinegar mixture.

Before latching the screen, we ventured to peep over the sill and look down at the dripping man clawing at his smarting eyes.

"He ought to be flogged for cussing like that on the church premises," remarked Carl. "Suppose we were to tell Brother Goodman about him?"

"He'd lose his job for such disgraceful conduct, wouldn't he?"

As we raced to an exit in the rear, we filled the musty corridors with guffaws that must have drained the place of all its termites.

CHAPTER FIVE

The Human Ramrod

When we scratched our hasty retreat over a high barbed fence that separated the church from a corn field to the south, we had no intention of returning to Sharkey's Ford until we were positive Mr. McKinney had gone home. But five minutes after we rasped our dusty way through the dry stalks and their tattling blades, we made a radical change in our intentions.

We would return to the scene of Foxy Mack's Waterloo, approaching from the direction of Main Street as if we had just left an uptown movie. If our victim was still there, we would let him tell us about his unpleasant experience and then we would offer to help him apprehend the culprits. He might suspect us to be the guilty ones, but his lack of incriminating evidence, added to our good standing with Brother Goodman, would doubtless prevent any attempt on his part to make an actual accusation.

"Bet you the ol' boy is in that rear room drying himself by the stove," Carl whispered when we observed that the light in our "study" was still burning.

"Lawrence," he added a moment later, "I've got another idea."

"Okay, do your worst."

"You're good at imitating ol' lady Andrews. Well, pal, here's your chance to put your impersonation into practical application."

"Let's have your plan, my fine-feathered Beebuzzard."

"Well, ten to one ol' Mack's in there with his clothes on some chairs next to the stove and naked as a pickaninny on wash day."

"Yeah, and trembling like a coon expelling peach seeds."

"Just because Mr. McKinny was a bit naughty when we splashed him with vinegar and salt water is no reason why we should be so crude here on these premises," said Carl in questionable seriousness after we had recovered from our ensuing spasms of suppressed laughter.

"Guy, we'd better hurry and get your scheme into action. Let's have the rest of it."

"Well, we'll rush down the hall, and as we get close to Mack's drying quarters, you'll raise your Mrs. Andrews voice and say: 'This is the room right here, Mrs. Goodman! I'm almost positive I left that magazine right in here!'"

"Boy, I can just see the ol' jay bird running for cover!"

"How'n heck would he explain such a situation, if we really were a couple of women?"

"Man, wouldn't that...."

A banging door slammed us into silence.

Satisfied that the janitor was coming down the hallway toward our place on the descending steps, Carl made another suggestion: "Let's run back to the other side of the canal and be walking this way when Mack ascends to the sidewalk!"

We met him under the street light.

"Hello, Mr. McPenny!" Carl sang cheerily.

"Hello, Mr. McSkinny!" I greeted. "What in the name of common sense have you been doing?"

An expression akin to self-pity snuggled on the short man's weatherworn face as he let his big optical lobes survey the wet corduroys clinging to his shaking limbs.

"I've been down there trying to dry myself," he answered, tossing his head toward the church.

"You must have fallen in the canal, Mr. McSkinny."

"Yep, yep, that's what it looks like happened, but it ain't. Somebody throwed a tub of water and stuff on me from that window over there." He raised his hand and pointed. "Cussed jokers almost put my eyes out."

"Who was it, Mr. McPenny?"

"I don't know, boys. But it must be them same fellers, whoever they was, that locked that goat up in the preacher's study last Saturday night. Took me an hour jist to clean up them pellets."

"Mr. McSkinny, a man who works as hard as you do ought to get a better salary." I was really sincere.

"You bet, Mr. McPenny. And the next time we have an opportunity to talk to any of the board of stewards, we're going to recommend a boost in your pay."

"Thank you, fellers. I always did figger I could count on you fellers."

"And by the way," said Sharkey, "you can count on us to help you catch the clout who soaked you tonight."

"You fellers think there was jist one?"

"Surely do, Mr. McPenny. And that one person was Jasper O. Rice. Do you know Jasper O. Rice?"

The old fellow, of course, didn't know the accused, for Jasper O. Rice was a nonentity existing solely in Beebuzzard imagination. Whenever we needed him for our amusement, Jasper was always ready to accommodate us. Once we even had him made song leader for a young peoples Christian organization. Of course, he was not present at the meeting, but our campaign speeches were impressive enough to give him an almost unanimous election. The members were quite disappointed when they received a letter from their new officer, who wrote that "pressing matters make it impossible for me to attend your little meetings, and so I must decline the honor of being your song leader."

"Lawrence," said Carl, "let's go in and nab that Jasper. I'll bet he's in there looking out at us right now. Come on, Mr. McPenny!"

Chilled to the bone, Foxy Mack shook along with us, pretending to be extremely grateful for our attempt to catch Jasper, who, according to us, was a half crazed degenerate capable of major violence as well as petty mischief.

We flooded the entire upper floor with lights and searched every nook and corner.

"Maybe, hereafter, I'd better git a license to tote a weapon," commented meditating Mack as we went cautiously down the creaking stairway to the quiet basement.

"Lawrence," said Carl, "I know exactly where that devil is hiding."

A moment later we were peering through the opening that gave view to our rat hole.

How could my buddy justify his revealing our cherished retreat? I wondered and waited for an answer.

"If I just had on my old clothes," mused Carl. "Yes, if only I had on some old clothes, I'd crawl back in there and see if he's there. How about you, Lefty? No, you've got on your good clothes, too. What a shame! But how about you, Mr. McPenny?"

"Well, boys, I...you...."

"Don't tell me you're afraid to go in there, Mr. McSkinny!"

"If you're afraid and fear prevents your doing your duty for your church, Mr. McPenny, I'm sorry to say we won't be able to recommend that extra pay for you, after all."

"No, no, I'm not scart."

"Well, come on, get the lead out, Mr. McPenny. Here's your flashlight. But whatever you do, don't turn it on until you're completely away from this opening; then he can't get you lined up against this outside light. See? See what I mean?"

The wet one didn't understand Carl's seemingly meaningless explanation, but he said disconcertedly: "Yep, yep," and Carl, who had loosened the bulb in the flashlight before handing it to its owner, was delighted.

"Now, Mr. McPenny, let's see you go in there and collar the rat who tried to drown you."

"Yep, but fellers, what if he's got himself a gun?"

"Well, that's exactly the reason why I told you not to turn on your flash until you get at least 15 or 18 feet from the background of light from the assembly room."

"Aw, fiddle," I contributed. "Suppose Jasper does have a gun? He's near-sighted, you know, and, moreover, it's too dark for him to draw a good bead on you."

"Courage, Mr. McPenny! Remember you are the guardian, the protector, the very champion for our church. If you fail us, Christianity itself fails, and when Christianity falls, the very timbers of civilization shatter!"

"You're certainly not going to let us and everybody else down, are you, Mr. McSkinny?"

Without waiting for a reply, we pushed the janitor through the dark aperture as if we were ramming a cleaning rod into a rifle barrel.

Above the man's muttered protests, Sharkey assured, "Why it'll be easy as taking tape off an Egyptian mummy, Mr. McPenny. And remember that when you're far enough back in there you can turn on your light and blind the sucker so he can't shoot straight."

Until Carl shut out the outside light by closing the closet door, we could see the dark form of our human bloodhound crawling slowly and hear the quiet patting of his knees against the soft earth.

"Okay, spear him with your flashlight, Mr. McPenny!"

From the rat hole came the sound of snaps and clicks made by Foxy Mack thumbing his unresponsive light.

At this point I tossed an old clay jar into the darkness and warned simultaneously: "Look out, Mr. Mack! He's coming toward you!"

In desperation the crawling one beat his faithless light against the ground, snarled an oath he tried too late to smother, and finally became frantic.

"Gimme some light, fellers!" he appealed in a shaky voice.

"Sorry, Mr. McPenny, but Jasper might be able to draw a bead on you, if we did. Just feel your way around and pounce on him. He's got you outweighed about 50 pounds and he's tough as a blackjack, but you've got right and justice on your side!"

"And right makes might, Mr. McSkinny," I threw in along with another jar.

"Look out, Mr. McPenny! There he comes!"

Thud. Our victim had wheeled too quickly and had allowed his head to remove some rust from one of the overhead pipes. He was less reserved with his profanity this time.

"I'm disappointed in you, Mr. McPenny. Do you think the Lord's going to be on your side after you've used that sort of language? He's liable to be on Jasper's side now. Be like Sir Galahad, whose strength was the strength of ten, because his heart was pure."

The janitor was silent.

Just as we were becoming concerned about him, we heard him scratching back into the closet.

"That you, boys?"

Carl shoved open the door and gave us some light.

"Boys, I sure am sorry I used them words. They jist leaked out. I ain't talked like that since I've been working at this church job. I would have apologized when I first said 'em, but that there fellow was jist too close and I shut up sos he wouldn't know where I was. Not that I was afraid, you understand."

Sharkey curled his lip for a fling of sarcasm but uncocked it when he had a better view of the janitor. The latter, his eyes bloodshot and watery, stood trembling with cold and stinking with vinegar. In places he was muddy and in other places he was slimy — slimy as a hog slopped on a dark night by a one-eyed drunkard.

Sorry for him, we hurried him to The Carcass, bundled him up in some old burlap sacks we found in the tool box and carried him home to his dismayed spouse.

And when we were sufficiently far enough away from Foxy Mack's habitation, we parked The Carcass and gave vent to laughter. It was the most we had laughed since that night before the Easter service when we shellacked the choir robes with brown Karo in invitation to banquet-bent sugar ants.

CHAPTER SIX

Sharkey Prays at the Parsonage

"Give it a few more turns," said Carl at my house a few weeks after the Foxy Mack episode.

We were freezing some well preserved sweet cider and wondering how it would taste. On other occasions we had tried freezing watermelon juice, buttermilk, and some other equally unappropriate liquids, all of which had proved unappetizing. But this was our first attempt at making cider ice cream.

When the handle on the old-fashioned freezer became sufficiently unyielding, we cleared the ice from around the container, detached the top of the apparatus and made an attack with a pair of eager tablespoons.

Sharkey, being the first to taste, was the first to leave the kitchen and donate his mouthful to the unsuspecting chickens, who pecked and cocked their heads and murmured and tried nobly to deceive themselves into believing the stuff was edible.

"My gosh, Lawrence! Did you ever taste anything so uninviting?"

"We must have put too much sodium benzoate in the cider," I suggested.

"Do you suppose we could take that taste out by adding some vanilla or something else?"

A measure of cocoa answered the question for us.

"Just goes to show," Carl gagged, "that a thing can always be made worse, no matter how bad it is."

In a desperate attempt to change the horrid flavor of the concoction, we added a touch of vanilla. It was no better, and so we introduced a modicum of orange extract and some coca cola.

Watching Tag, my old bob-tailed hound, as he sampled a cup of the mixture, Carl said, "Boy, that's a brave brute! He's got plenty of guts now, but he won't have later, if he eats much of that stuff."

"That poor mutt. I thought he had more sense."

"Look at him shake. Reminds me of Foxy Mack. Lawrence, he can't like that ungodly mess; he's just eating to please us. He's just like...." Sharkey's face became radiant.

"Say, guy, I've got an idea," he said, a mischievous gleam in his eyes.

"Let's have it, lad."

"Here's our chance to see if Mrs. Goodman compliments just everybody, no matter what they do."

"I think I see what you mean. If she tried this disgrace to creamhood and says it's good, we'll know she's insincere even when she compliments us on our talks at Epworth League."

"Right!"

Lest my parents return from a visit to the neighbors and find the kitchen in too much of a disarray, we stirred hurriedly about the place in a pretense at tidying it up. But I'm afraid that when we loaded the freezer in the Model T, we left behind a kitchen that bristled with disorder as though it had housed a steer who had caught his tail in the heated grate of the cooking range.

We found plump, rosy-cheeked Mrs. Goodman working in her back yard.

"You're just in time to help with the raking," she intoned with kindling laughter that unveiled a set of lovely uppers.

"We'll try to bribe our way out with some ice cream we brought you, Mrs. Goodman," said Sharkey.

"Ice cream for me?"

"A whole gallon," I responded wrestling with the rattling freezer in an attempt to remove it from the Model T without spilling the water and ice around the container.

"It's so warm and nice outside," said our hostess, an ardent outdoors enthusiast, "I'll bring some spoons and saucers outside and we'll just have a real picnic."

"Isn't Brother Goodman here?" I inquired. "We want him in on this, too."

"Well, yes, he's here, but he's taking his regular afternoon nap, and I'd rather not disturb him. But we'll save some for him and Mother Goodman when they get up."

"Did you make that angel food cake, Mrs. Goodman?" asked my accomplice.

The pastor's wife nodded, pushed back a few annoying strands of blonde hair and cut another piece of the air-conditioned pastry.

"I'll bet you're as proud of that cake as we are of this ice cream," I contributed, watching Carl build a miniature skyscraper on a third saucer. "This is the result of our own recipe, you know."

"That's an odd color," our victim remarked, scrutinizing the brown mess Carl handed her. "What flavor is it?"

"See if you can guess," instructed Carl. To help himself hold a sober countenance, he stuffed his mouth full of cake and I concealed a grin with my faithful handkerchief.

The lady's face glowed with happy anticipation as her thumb and three fingers, accompanied by a sophisticated little one that curled up like a deformed appendix, conveyed a generous helping of "ice cream" to an eager palate.

But on the palate the helping suddenly halted and lingered precariously awaiting orders from Mrs. Goodman, whose facial features had taken a sudden nose-dive.

Carl ruined our opportunity to put her sincerity to a real test when he lost control of himself and squealed in unbridled merriment.

When the grimacing Mrs. Goodman forgot her culture and raucously spit out the unwelcome helping, Carl dropped haw-hawing to the ground and was floundering in a mound of ashes when he choked on cake crumbs.

Beating the latter on the back of his ash-flying jacket while he coughed his face into an almost poker-end redness, I was almost glad that the joke had backfired, for Carl was to blame for its untimely failure.

When he and the pastor's wife had finished laughing at one another and I had finished laughing at both of them, the good-natured woman ushered us into the parsonage parlor and delighted us with: "Now you boys make yourselves at home while I stir up some egg custard, and we'll have some ice cream yet."

To settle the question whether we would search the nearby radio dial for Hawaiian music, which was Carl's favorite, or organ music, my favorite, we tossed a coin.

"You're just not living right, Lawrence," my buddy said with a grin as he pocketed his dime and reached for one of the walnut knobs.

The polished cabinet squealed statically as if it resented being fingered by a Beebuzzard.

"Good afternoon!"

The voice was strong despite its 92-year-old owner, who had stolen quietly upon us from her bedroom adjoining the parlor.

Carl snapped off the static, for it would be hard enough to make Brother Goodman's mother understand us, without having additional noise.

"How are you, Mother Goodman?" I asked of the thin, white-topped lady now folding herself into a fat rocker.

"Now let me see," she mused, ignoring my inquiry. "Who is this speaking?"

"Mother Goodman, I'm Lawrence Nelson and this is Carl Lewis," I replied almost loudly. "We're officers in the Epworth League." It was about the fifth time we or somebody else had introduced us since the family's arrive in March.

"Oh, yes, of course," the oldster responded in a vain attempt to make us believe she had recalled our identities.

"Well," she continued after a pause, "I suppose you are wondering why I don't have some spectacles on my nose. Well, you see, I'm getting my second eye-sight. Uh...huh." Her "uh...huh," prolonged and almost musical, was an attachment she seemed always fond of suffixing to her utterances.

"Well, sir, when my second eyesight arrives completely, I'll be able to recognize everybody just as soon as he comes in. Uh...huh, and maybe I'll be able to read again, too."

"Mother Goodman, do you have any sons other than Brother Goodman? Carl had beaten me to the question we always asked the old one each time we were introduced to her.

It was a sort of game with us Beebuzzards. She would tell us that she had a minister son and a lawyer son, and then just as she started to add, "I should have had a doctor son," we would "beat her to the punch," as Sharkey put it.

"Uh...huh," she hummed. "I have two sons in all. One is a minister and the other is a lawyer. I should...."

"You should have had a doctor son, shouldn't you?" we interrupted to say in unison.

We hoped she wouldn't become discouraged. Let her take hope, for sometime she might catch us off guard and finish her line herself.

The sound of her pounding rocking chair covered up Carl's snicker.

"Carl," I reproved, "you're losing your will power."

"Will who?" said Mother Goodman, cupping a hand behind one ear as if to indicate her hearing was poor.

An opening door diverted our attention to Brother Goodman, who was coming forward to exercise his Sunday-go-to-meeting handshake.

"Glad to see you, Carl and Lawrence," he beamed. He blew his distinguishingly pointed nose, made a couple of digs at it with his handkerchief, and dropped into a chair opposite the divan in which we reseated ourselves.

"I hope we didn't wake you up before you finished your nap," I said to the preacher, who was running his bony fingers through a well preserved tuft of dark hair that would have been frosty but for seasonal doses of dye.

Unlike his plump wife, he was thin. The first time I had seen him and her together I saw their situation as being quite contrary to that of Jack Sprat, who "could eat no fat," and his wife, who "could eat no lean."

"No, I was through. In fact, I almost slept overtime."

A few minutes later, when the custard was ready to be frozen, Brother and Mrs. Goodman retired with us to the back porch, where we Beebuzzards hung alternately on the freezer crank.

Carl was turning and I was conversing with the minister when the latter noticed that a neighbor's white leghorn hen had left her owner's yard and was meandering about the parsonage lawn.

"Now there's Brother Ranger's old hen in here again," he fretted.

"Well, my goodness, let the old chicken peck around," said Mrs. Goodman. "How can she possibly hurt anything?"

"Well, it's just the principle of the thing I don't like. I noticed Brother Ranger kept her in his own yard until recently. And now that Thanksgiving is so close, he's turned her in here so she can eat our scraps and get fat for his Thanksgiving table."

A fleck of gold in a front tooth added zest to the churchman's grin and then played peek-a-boo at me as he said, "Lawrence, your mother surely does have a lot of lovely looking fryers. I was just admiring them a few days ago when I drove by. I suppose you'll have plenty of delicious fried chicken for Thanksgiving, won't you?"

"Yes, sir, I guess we will."

"My, my," said the fryer enthusiast, "but I'm fond of fried chicken. I was just telling Marjorie last week there's nothing I like better than fried chicken...that is, when I know the owner has taken good care of the bird. I can't enjoy cold storage fowl, but my, my, how I like...."

It would have made Mrs. Goodman unhappy to know that I saw her pulling the end of the ice cracker from her husband's ribs.

"We're going to have turkey this year," she said, laying the cracker on the table. "And there isn't anything better than that."

"My, my that's wonderful, Marjorie!" exclaimed Brother Goodman. "Who's giving it to us?"

"Why, Clyde, we're going to buy it. I've already spoken to...."

"Marjorie, don't you realize how expensive turkeys are? No, I'm sorry we can't afford that kind of bird."

Creeping upon us from the rear, Mother Goodman heard the last word and said, "Yes, that mockingbird has been singing all day. Uh...huh. Doesn't he have a beautiful voice?"

"But, Clyde, Thanksgiving comes but once a year. We can surely have one to eat then."

"Uh...huh. What? Eat a mockingbird!"

"No, no, mother. Marjorie is talking about a turkey."

"Somebody brought us a turkey?"

"No, Mother Goodman, Clyde is going to have to buy it."

"Oh, I see. Uh...huh. But how much does one cost?"

"Too much, mother. But now if some good member were to bring us a good...."

"Is the cream getting hard, boys?" asked the preacher's spouse, purposely drowning out her husband's sentence and simultaneously picking up the cracker, which she hoped would be unnoticed by any except her Clyde.

"It won't be too long now, Mrs. Goodman," said Carl.

"What's too long?" inquired the addressee's mother-in-law.

"Mother Goodman," said the daughter-in-law, "don't you think it's a little chilly out here for you? You'd better go in and sit in the front room."

About 80 turnings later we, too, returned to the parlor where we sat to eat the delicious custard and some more of the hostess' cake.

Feeling that I was on the outskirts of a discussion involving a subject common only to the minister, his wife, and Carl, Mother Goodman turned to me and said: "Do you know my granddaughter Alice?"

"Oh, yes ma'am. I've been knowing her since last March. Have you heard from her lately, by the way?"

"Uh...huh. She's coming home sometime...Christmas, I guess. She goes away to college, you know. Uh...huh."

I looked at the 8 by 10 photograph of Brother and Mrs. Goodman's daughter as it smiled up at me from the coffee table. She was somewhat pretty, but not beautiful, by any means. There was something about Alice that attracted me, and although I would not admit the fact to anyone, I rather looked forward to the freshman's return for the Yuletide season.,

"I've got two grandsons, but Alice is my only granddaughter."

"How many children do you have, Mother Goodman?"

Apparently she did not remember that she had answered that question earlier in the afternoon, for she showed neither confusion nor hesitation.

"I don't have any daughters, but I have two sons. Uh...huh. One is a minister, and another one is a lawyer. I should...."

"You should have had a doctor son, shouldn't you?" Carl broke in.

Confound my fellow Beebuzzard! But how was he to know that I meant to give the old lady this opportunity to finish her line?

Had he known, he might have wondered why I had suffered this moment of weakness, and I would never have told him that the reason was the face on the coffee table. Yes, there was something about the girl that brought out the noble in me. Once, for instance, learning that she was going to be in the Easter morning congregation, I abandoned my plan to place a whoopee cushion camouflaged in gingham in her father's pulpit chair.

When we had stretched our stomachs to full capacity, Carl brushed some crumbs from his lap and reminded me that if we were going to keep our handball engagement with a pair of Hispanic players at the junior high school building, we ought to be leaving.

"Well, boys, before you go," said the minister. "shall we have some sentence prayers? Marjorie, suppose you begin, and Carl will you ring in the conclusion?"

"All right, Clyde," answered the spouse. "Shall we bow our heads?"

With the single exception of Mother Goodman, who had evidently failed to understand her son's suggestion, we all tilted our faces floorward and Mrs. Goodman began with: "Our dear Heavenly Maker, we beseech thee...."

"Bake a peach pie!" interrupted the 92-year-old. "Oh, that will be lovely. Uh...huh."

"Please, Mother Goodman," elucidated the pastor's wife, "we're having sentence prayers."

"Oh, excuse me! I'm so sorry. Uh...huh."

Brother Goodman prayed next, and then came my time.

Finally, in a most reverent tone, Carl concluded our supplications with: "Our dear Heavenly Father, we thank thee for health and life and all thou hast given us. We thank thee especially for conscience, that inner voice that helps us to be Christians and inspires us to be good neighbors and charitable in our dealings with our fellow man. We want always, Oh Lord, to be kind to each and every person with whom we are concerned. Guide us and bless us. Amen."

"Amen!" assented the clergyman.

We shook his hand, thanked our hostess for a most enjoyable visit, and took our leave.

While we jolted along two blocks in the Ford, Carl looked up to the blue heavens above and I meditated upon the beautiful prayer he had offered. Did the contents of that prayer mean that he was not going to play pranks again? Couldn't one play pranks and still be neighborly? Looking now into the sky, was he glorying in his transformation and in a probably resolution henceforward to treat God's human beings with more kindness? Things might be different from now on, I suspected. Perhaps now our escapades would become mere memories and we would pursue the ordinary track of other youths. Well, maybe it was all for the best. Now I could look Alice straight in the eyes and know that my present at least was free of further mischief.

"Lawrence," said Carl, at last breaking in on my somber thinking, "you know, an old crow I was watching overhead a minute ago left me with a thought."

"Yes," I sighed. Although this modification of ourselves was doubtless to be desired, it was, nevertheless, somehow a bit sad to me. The name Beebuzzard would have to be replaced by a more dignified and refined appellation. It would decease; it would be buried in the catacombs of our eventful yesterdays.

"Well, I've got a suggestion to make," Carl continued after a pause.

"Go ahead, Carl." I started to address him as "Sharkey," but thought it better to let his nickname go along with our Royal Society of the Beebuzzards.

"Let's get our rifles, kill a crow, dress it, and send it with a note reading: 'Brother Goodman, I'm sending you this nice fryer for your Thanksgiving dinner.' And, by golly, we'll sign Mr. McKinney's name!"

"Long live the Beebuzzards!" was my spontaneous outburst, and Sharkey echoed the cry.

CHAPTER SEVEN

We Take Snerd for a Ride

On the night previous to Christmas Eve, we were sitting quietly absorbed in a movie when the toe-headed objects of our sarcastic poem wagged ostentatiously down the theater aisle and seated themselves directly in front of us.

Sight of the blonde pair must have reminded my companion, as it did me, of our editor friend's refusal to publish our satire. Confound him! Didn't he recognize a literary gem when he saw one?

Perhaps we might yet have to resort to sending it by mail to the girls. But, for the time being, we would wait with the hope that our editor would relent and give our work the circulation we were sure it deserved.

Coming in during the middle part of the film, the toe-heads naturally did not fully appreciate the scenes in progress and therefore talked to the extent of disturbing us; to annoy us, however, was not their design, for they believed us too socially insignificant to merit their consideration. Adding to our irritation was the younger girl's meager hat that sported a plume seemingly intent on reaching toward the artificial stars that hung from the blue ceiling.

Trust Carl to have an idea about this time.

Let's go back and arm ourselves," he said in an unconcealed impatience.

At the confectionery in the lobby we each bought a sack of popcorn and a chocolate bar encased in cellophane. Now that we had our weapons, we started back down the thick carpet.

As we neared the dual sources of our revengeful mood, Carl uttered a couple of impromptu verses he had been composing, lines whose meter was shared by "The Campus Flirts":

"With crumple, crumple here we're back
With cellophane and popcorn sack."

To our joy the blondes had now become engrossed in the film and were silent.

It was still that era when kisses on the screen were endurance contests, when each fire-eyed lover seemed bent on tasting whatever the other had last eaten.

"The two sand-tops regard us as yokels," my buddy said scornfully, "and so let's not disappoint them."

"Okay, lad."

Loud so that they could hear, Carl grumbled in reference to the actor and actress. "Look at them critters, Lefty. Look at 'em heaving and puffing, their lips suckin' one another like two plumber's friends."

"Yeah, haw haw! Ain't they playin' the devil though?"

And now we rustled the candy wrappers close to the toe-heads' ears.

At last one of them turned around and speared us with an Amazon gleam that would have surely daunted anyone but a Beebuzzard.

"We was here first, sister," I snarled.

"And besides," reinforced my ally, "ain't this here a free country?"

"She must be like one o' them dictatoe fellers, I heard about."

"Lefty, that ain't the way to pronounce that word. Pronounce it *dickatator.*"

"How'n heck you know? You ain't so pert."

"That's all right, my Uncle Jasper O. Rice told me how to pronounce 'at word and, gosh, about ten or twelve otha big words!"

"Who the heck is Jasper O. Rice?"

"Lefty, you mean to sit there in yore ventilated flannels and tell me you ain't heard of Jasper O. Rice? Why, he's a right smart feller. Got a M. A., he has."

"Well, pshaw, I got a ma, too. Who ain't? That ain't nothin' extry ordinary."

The enemy could endure our rustic warfare no longer.

"Sis," said one, condescending to send a contemptuous glance our way, "let's go sit somewhere else and get out of this noisy trash!"

"High-flutin' babes, ain't they!" Carl called after them.

"Aw, shucks, they left 'fore we et our corn and popped some sacks!"

The show over, we made for Crockett Drug, where we instructed Al to bring two phosphates up the steps to the raised gallery overlooking the fountain. Beebuzzard Roost, we called it, for it was a suitable retreat for us when we would partake of refreshments and scan and scoff at an occasional enemy being served below.

We were just about to order refills when Carl cast an eye downward and said, "Do you see what I see?"

Bernard Snerd with Alice Goodman," I mumbled slowly, but not with indifference.

"Do you suppose her old man knows about this?"

"Why certainly, Sharkey. But why should he object to Alice's going with the clout? He doesn't know him as we do."

"That's a funny thing how a reprobate can deceive some people so successfully."

"Why, heck, Brother Goodman thinks Bernard's the stuff. I heard him say not so long ago, `My, my, but Bernard is a fine young man. It's not every young fellow that would come to church and sing in the evening choir.' "

"Funny about that. Wonder if he was hinting that we ought to sing in the choir, or wonder if he was insinuating Snerd isn't a prankster like us?"

"Been drinking," I observed.

"Yep. His favorite activity nearly every night except Sunday. Yes sir, fine young fellow. Stays sober Sunday night so he can warble in the church."

"Carl, are we going to sit here and let him get in that hack of his in a few minutes and drive Alice out on the mesa to his usual seduction grounds?"

"We wouldn't be good Christians, if we did, would we?"

I had two reasons for assuming leadership in this, our latest stratagem. In the first place, I knew that Alice's security meant a bit more to me than it did to my buddy. In the second place, I thought it was about time that I did something to disprove Carl's recent contention that I left "all the dirty work" to him.

"Lad," I proposed, "let's carry our glasses downstairs and while Al's filling `em up, we'll casually begin a conversation with Alice. You hold that conversation, and I'll go out and attend to her boyfriend's Oldsmobile."

"Quite so, ol' chap," agreed Carl, in an Oxford English brogue. "Pregnant idea! Simply pregnant, don't you know. But I dare say, ol' Cheroot, ol' garbage heap, ol'...."

"Eh, wot, ol' vulture?"

"I was about to say, ol' chap, it's a beastly night for this Snerd fellow to be walking home — frightfully chilly wind and all that ol' rot, don't cha know?"

"But, my deah Sir Carl, we shall return for him as soon as we convey the damsel to her abode."

"Quite so. And if I might be so bold as to say, ol' sock, he shall have a jolly ol' time of it ere he reaches his own abode. Right, ol' boy?"

"Right, ol' boy."

"Then lead on, ol' boy. Let us to our noble administration."

Alice, her personality gleaming in blue eyes that floated warmly among brown curls, flashed a very friendly smile at us and greeted: "The two musketeers! Gee, but it's swell to see you fellas always together. It keeps up my faith in friendship."

Observing the friendliness his date had extended, Snerd descended from his usual balcony of social superiority and pleased her by inviting us to join them "in a coke."

"We'll just take a coupla cherry phosphates, if you don't mind," Sharkey returned stonily.

"Coke too strong for you guys?" This from the drinking one.

"No, we just like to see the pretty red color in phosphates." Sometimes when Carl indulged in sarcasm, a ridge like a smeared comma would appear in his left cheek and seem to play tag with his nose that for the moment would descend to complete a beautiful sneer. The punctuation mark was there now.

Sensing the unneighborly feeling we bore for Snerd, Alice tactfully began to talk about the show we had just seen.

"I'd thought I'd die laughing," she said, "when Clark Gable came in and...Lawrence, what in the world are you sniffing at?"

"Alcohol, Alice," I dared. "The whole place smells like a saloon. Does it grace your nostrils, Sharkey?"

"I'll say it does. If I were a drinking Scotchman, I'd just open my nose and get sopping drunk."

"I'm safe," Snerd chuckled. "I got a bad case of adenoids."

"Haw, haw, haw," fleered my buddy in mock sincerity. "Did you hear that, Lefty? Alice, your escort is a wit. Yea, a ha...."

The nudge I had given Carl probably prevented the occurrence of a nasty scene. It was quite possible that he of the erectile mustache would have resented Carl's appending "half wit."

In the background someone had inserted a nickel in a hungry slot and pushed a button and now from the dusty juke box a canned vocalist, like a phantom jack-in-a-box, seemed to spring forth to croon:

> "Stay as sweet as you are
> And as you are;
> You're divine, dear...."

Alice would stay as sweet as she was, I vowed silently, consumed for the moment by a very youthful feeling of heroism that inspired me to liken the Beebuzzards unto the Arthurian knights of the Round Table.

"Oh, by the way, Alice," I said, at last thinking of a way to leave the three here to converse while I attended to Snerd's vehicle outside, "I have those snapshots of the League picnic we made last fall just before you left for school. They're out in Sharkey's car. Want to see them?"

"Oh, yes!"

"Then hold everything and I'll be back with them in a twink."

"Swell!"

Carl rose automatically, but I eyed him back down. This was my mission.

To be positive that the owlish night watch or one of his spying bootblacks was not in the vicinity of the maroon Oldsmobile, I stood shadowed under a flapping awning long enough to survey the street. Except for a trio stepping northward from the theater, it was, for the moment, a ghost town.

The 40,000 must have been praying for me, for no one saw me lean over the enemy's motor, pull out some ignition wires from their distributor sockets and return them insulated with strips of a paper napkin.

But suppose Snerd was something of a mechanic? He might soon find the cause of his trouble and soon be en route to the open spaces with his Methodist freshman.

Well, the valve core of the rear right tire yielded cooperatively enough, but the stem was a regular Paul Revere trying to whistle the entire neighborhood to arms against an invader Beebuzzard.

The 40,000 were evidently still on their knees, for the street remained peopleless, even while Snerd's spare became breathless.

Alice was disappointed when I came back to say that we must have misplaced the snapshots.

"Here's hoping you find them before the holidays are over," she said.

Her escort, whose liquor by now was beginning to wrestle with his tongue, rose and driveled, "Les go, kiddo, ol' girl. We gotta go, and when we gotta go...well, we gotta."

"On one condition, Bernardy."

"What, kiddo?"

"Well, you're going to let me drive, aren't you? I've just been dying to get behind the wheel of that big Olds!"

"Well, okay. Like I said, if you gotta, you gotta."

Alice made no attempt to hide an expression that seemed to say: "Whew! What a relief; I was afraid he'd want to drive, and he's in no condition to drive."

They had been gone perhaps 15 minutes when the girl came back to query: "Say, do either of you two know anything about an Oldsmobile? We can't get Bernard's car started."

We found Snerd bracing himself with a vertical flask.

"A man's gotta have somepin to keep himsel' warm," he explained, a bit embarrassed that the preacher's daughter should catch him in his indulgence.

After Sharkey ran the battery down, I raised the hood and removed the bits of insulating napkin. Why take a chance on the possibility of Snerd's eventually finding such incriminating evidence?

All the while, our drinking acquaintance had merely sat on the front seat and divided his speech between railing his "stinky hack" and thanking us for "being susch swell pals."

"Well, Snerd," decided Carl, "looks as if we'll have to take Alice home in our wreck."

"Wup, wup. Now hold everything, pal! I got friends, see? I can get somebody to fiss this hack, and I'll take Alice home. See? You think I'm gonna let this sweet kiddo go home in an ol' Model T?"

"What's the matter with a Model T?" I flared indignantly and then quickly realized that Alice was listening and would resent a scene, particularly one here on Main Street.

"Now, if you can't see the dif in a big shiny Olds and a...."

"You can't get a garageman," my buddy interposed, "to fix your starter trouble and charge your battery at this late hour, Snerd."

"And you've got that flat tire too, Bernard, don't forget," Alice reminded.

"I know, Kiddo. I know. And I'm gonna change that right...."

"What's the trouble, Snerd?" I asked of the self-interrupted inebriate, who was pounding on his airless spare.

"The spare's flat, too!" he squalled. "Whatta lotta rotten breaks! Battery down, flat tire, flat spare, garages all closed, cold as a bear trap. Shoot, I been livin' like a Chrishun. Why I gotta get all this in the neck like this?" He reached for his hip pocket but let his hand fall when he remembered the minister's offspring.

Ten minutes later Alice and we Beebuzzards were bumping along in the direction of the parsonage. Insisting that there wasn't room in the coupe for Snerd, we had coaxed him into remaining with the Oldsmobile until we should return to take him home.

"You know," Alice remarked meditatively, "it's kinda funny Bernard had all that trouble at once. Two flats and engine trouble. It's just too coincidental."

"It is rather strange," agreed Carl. "You know, Lefty," he said looking at me, "the whole thing assumes the aspect of a first-class Sunday-go-to-meetin' bit of foul play. Right?"

"Right."

Both of us realized simultaneously that Alice might always suspect that her escort had fallen victim to a malicious bit of deviltry, and both of us sought to name the suspect lest our pondering coed should begin casting suspicious thoughts Beebuzzard way.

"Well," said Carl, "the case, as I see it, bears the earmarks of a Jasper O. Rice deal."

"Jasper O. Rice — that's our man," I supported.

"Who's Jasper O. Rice? What's he got against Bernard?"

"Alice, do you mean to say you've never heard of Jasper O. Rice?" Carl's tone overflowed with amazement.

"Seems to me I've heard that name lately, but I can't remember when or where? Who is he, anyway?"

Carl undertook the identification: "Well, he's a short, thin, sickly sort of kid of about 16 whose hobby consists in making other people miserable."

"Well, gee whiz, why don't the police put him in a reform school or something?"

"Thus far, he's been too smart for them," I explained. "Lots of people know he's the town's ne'er-do-well, but he's too clever to be caught in any of his meanness."

"Say, now I remember that name!" exclaimed Alice.

She swallowed, pulled her scarf closer to her neck, and continued with: "Well, daddy told me that about a day or two before Thanksgiving an old Hispanic man came to the door and delivered a package. Daddy asked him who it was from, but the old man couldn't speak English. Well, daddy was about to unwrap it when he noticed a note bearing his church janitor's name and saying that he was sending a nice fryer for daddy's Thanksgiving dinner."

"Well, now that was nice of Mr. McSkinney."

"Oh, but it wasn't a fryer, at least it surely didn't look like one. Daddy said if it was, it must have died with T.B. or starved to death."

"Mr. McPenny ought to be ashamed of himself."

"Oh, but the janitor said he didn't send the thing, whatever it was. He said this Jasper or somebody else — he hadn't decided which — had thrown some acid in his face one night last fall and that it might have been the same party that sent this dried-up fowl."

Alice forgot her seriousness, however, and laughed with us at Sharkey's comment: "Mr. McPenny's eyes aren't so dependable, you know; maybe he mistook a squab for a chicken and then wouldn't admit his blunder."

After we saw the Goodman's lighted Christmas tree and promised Alice we'd not tell her parents what the tree and Bernard had in common, we jogged back to the Oldsmobile and transferred its half-conscious occupant to our "limousine."

"Where you guys taking me?" he muttered in harmony with his flask grumbling hollowly on the vibrating floorboard.

"Why, we're taking you home, of course, Snerd," I replied.

"Well, where's my car? Huh, Nelson?"

"We couldn't get it started. Don't you remember?"

"Course, I remember. You think I'm crazy? Don't you think I got a mind o' my own?"

"Why, certainly you have, Snerd. You've got some kind of a mind, no doubt."

"You guys are my pals. I don' aim to forget that. Sharkey?"

"Yes?"

"Don' let me forget that. You guys are my pals. Yeah, an' I used to think you guys were a coupla stuffed shirts. Anybody `at says `at is got me to fight. You think I can't fight, Lefty? You're crazy. Yeah, you're my pal, Lefty. So're you, Sharkey. Say, what's the matter? Where's my car? This not my car!"

Five miles out of town, we stopped the coupe, slipped a rope around the waist of our slumbering inebriate, shook his listless eyes open, and told him to get out.

"Huh? What's matter?"

"Get out, Snerd," reiterated Carl.

"What's goin' on? We home?"

"We're your pals, Snerd," I explained, "and you know a pal doesn't take a pal home while he's drunk. What would your sister Betsy have to say if you came home drunk? By the way, why didn't your sister's marriage go through as planned?"

"You guys are crazy if you think I'm tight!"

As we pulled the rope and drew him toward the moonlit drainage canal it was hard to determine which was the tighter, the lasso or the resisting bundle it encircled.

But by the time we reached the sandy bank, the cold air and the struggle had restored some of Snerd's thinking power.

"This looks like foul play to me!" he suggested. "What've I ever done to you guys? I didn't do anything. Betsy was the one that always said you were nuts — I didn't!"

He grunted a few steps, looked alarmed at a tall cottonwood tree, and yelled: "Help! Help, somebody! They're gonna hang me!"

"We're not going to hang you, Snerd. We're just going to sober you up by dousing you in this canal. Isn't that right, Lefty?"

"That's right. You ought to appreciate this, Snerd. How many other friends do you have who'd expose themselves to this cold air and risk taking pneumonia just to sober you up like this?"

"Some people just don't appreciate anything," said Carl as he gave our patient a shove that sent him splashing to the stagnant mess below.

"Ug!" grunted the latter, rising strangled to the surface and beating the water to keep his mouth afloat.

"I can't swim!" he finally managed to appeal.

"Don't worry, Snerd!" I comforted. "We've got you on a rope — you won't drown!"

Each time I shoved him back into his murky bath, I would say soothingly, "Bernard Snerd, I disbaptize thee in the name of the devil, the 40,000 angels of Hades, and the Royal Society of the Beebuzzards."

Soon after the floundering one's third emersion, he caught hold of a black something, threw his arms about it, and ceased to paddle.

"He's found some kind of a lifesaver," I observed. "Looks like a big log."

At that instant Brother Goodman's "fine young man" turned himself loose in a spree of violent oaths.

Simultaneously Carl shrieked in merriment, stopping only long enough to squeal: "He must've thought we had thrown him an innertube...until he got the water out of his nose!"

Then finally I saw it in a place where the light was better — the floating carcass of a bloated hog.

CHAPTER EIGHT

Cousin Boyd's Capers in Church

"How are you, Cousin Boyd?" I inquired of my dried-up relative just after Sunday School a month after Santa Claus, or *somebody* had left him a can of itching powder labeled "Talcum Ointment."

"I'm in bad shape, son — bad shape."

It was the old story, the one I had been hearing from his tabacco-clad lips since my early boyhood.

"Yeah, these fool doctors can't do me any good, Lawrence. They don't know anything. It's like I told...."

Here he stopped and coughed until his underslung nose stood out on his rosy but sour face like a red handle on a pink flower vase.

"Step back here with me, son," he invited with a nod toward the church alley. "Well sir, Dr. Hogue told me to take a little snorta brandy every time this cough gets to ticklin' my throat. Well, son, I know how you stand on the liquor issue, but you know when your doctor tells you to do somethin' you gosh dern better do it."

"Cousin Boyd, doesn't that stuff aggravate your stomach ulcer?"

"Now you sound like that gosh dern Dr. Hogue. Know what that fool told me, Lawrence? Said alcohol was part of my trouble. But it's like I told you: You can't pay much attention to what these doctors say. Why, Lawrence, this stuff's my medicine! When then blamed insides of mine get stubborn like they're always doing, this stuff sorta stimulates 'em. It sure helps my cough, too."

Seeing that I was looking back at the sidewalk, my cousin assured me: "You don't need worry, son; those folks are not gonna see us and think you're back here taking' a swig with me. Nope...the women are all too busy lookin' at one another's hats, and the men are all too busy lookin' at the women's legs."

He of the stubborn "insides" dropped his brandy container in with his small Bible in the pocket of his blue serge coat and pulled out a long slab of tobacco.

"Nothing like this for a chaser," he remarked, and for an instant he seemed on the verge of indulging in a smile, a thing which for several years had been foreign to his countenance.

In spite of Cousin Boyd's loud chewing, I heard the sound of Carl's Model T and excused myself to go to the main church entrance, where the Beebuzzards had promised to meet at 10:45.

We were going up the steps together and my buddy was explaining the plans he had made for his Epworth League program for that night when suddenly his voice was overcast by a raucous fanfare of nose blowing and a retinue of violent coughs.

"Hello, Lewis and Nelson," Bernard Snerd greeted, after the microbes grew weary of sandpapering his tonsils. That cool formality and that old aloofness of his were back again.

"Son," said a voice from behind, "you oughta try some of my medicine for that throat."

Since the morning service would not begin until 11:00, the auditorium was uncrowded enough to allow the four of us to choose choicy seats. Bernard took a place in the left section, we Beebuzzards sat down toward the rear of the center section, and Cousin Boyd made for his usual seat just two rows in front of us.

There, however, he stopped and frowned down at Mother Goodman.

"Madam," he said in a low voice, "that's my pew."

"I'm fine, and how are *you?*" responded she of the aged ears.

"I say, madam, you have my pew."

"And a cordial howdy do to you, too. Uh...huh."

"You don't understand. This is my seat...this one, the one you're sitting' in — it's mine!"

With her understanding came a question: "Did you buy it?"

"No, but I've been sitting here for 15 years, and everybody knows it!"

"My, but that's a long time to be sitting in one place, Uh...huh. Aren't you afraid you'll wear it out?"

"Lefty, I'll bet that cousin of yours has been tilting his medicine bottle," whispered Carl.

Loud enough now so that a score of listeners did not have to strain their auditory organs, Cousin Boyd bent low and delivered to the pastor's mother an ultimatum: "Madam, if you don't move over and let me have my niche here next to the aisle, I'm gonna report this case to Brother Goodman and the board of trustees, and, if they don't get action, I'll take my membership and financial support to some other church."

"Young man," replied Mother Goodman to my 53-year-old relative, "you can see the President of the United States and I still won't move, but if you just say, 'Please,' I'll let you have your ol' seat."

Doubtless it was the feather of Providence that tickled Cousin Boyd's nose at this time and made him sneeze, for Mother Goodman, mistaking the sneeze for 'Please!' moved five feet to her right and said, "All right, young man, here's your seat. And I hope my son will say something in his sermon today to reach your soul. Uh...huh."

A few minutes after my kinsman had dropped his bony finger into a collection plate to jostle the coins and deceive, as usual, his neighbors into believing he had made a contribution, the minister began his morning prayer. It was toward the end of this prayer when Cousin Boyd, who was always an eager sleeper, began to snore.

"Lefty, it's your Christian duty to stop that," Carl asserted in a whisper as he handed me a rubber band and a strip of tinfoil from a Hersey bar.

"But, Sharkey, you're a better marksman than I."

"Oh, but he's your cousin, not mine."

"Okay. But I'd rather not pop him right now. We don't want him to yell out as he did when we let him have it during Brother Goodman's benediction last summer."

"You're right. Let's wait until the next song and do it in the usual way."

Came the amen pronouncement and its noisy caboose of throats that were cleared, feet that were shifted, joints that were snapped, and semi-numb rumps that were readjusted on the adamantine benches.

"While we are turning to Hymn 25, I want to say," said the voice in the pulpit, "that we're so happy to have our fine young friend, Mr. Bernard Snerd, back with us again after his recent illness. Bernard assured the pastor that one of the most regretful features of his confinement was his inability to attend church services and participate in the evening choir activities. It's a real inspiration to work with such a fine Christian young man."

As we rose with the congregation to sing "Revive Us Again," Carl slipped his right thumb through the circular elastic band and held his half of the book with both hands while I slipped my left thumb through the other end of the band and grasped my part of the book. With my free hand I bent the tinfoil missile over the flexible band and pulled it back along the crease of the hymnal.

No one was between us and our mark, and so as we sang, we lowered the farther end of our "crossbow" until it was aligned even with a spot midway between my cousin's jack rabbit ears.

Anticipating his reaction, I deliberately waited until we came to the chorus and just as we burst loudly into "Hallelujah!" I released the restless foil. With lightning speed it hissed down its ecclesiastical runway and flattened out against its target.

Like a gigantic frog, he of the obstinate abdominal region flung his hands above his shoulder and leaped to his feet with a frantic cry that might have been quite disturbing to the congregation had not we Beebuzzards borne down rather heavily on "Thine the glory!"

To Mother Goodman, the man's outburst was a sudden manifestation of religious enthusiasm.

I saw her smile and read her lips when she leaned toward Cousin Boyd and said, "Young man, I believe you've got the Holy Ghost, and I'm glad for you."

The pastor had announced his theme, "Moved by the Spirit of the Lord," and was reading a series of scriptures when my cousin stopped massaging his head and rose pale of face and with a grimace that worried me into following him to inquire about his apparently serious condition.

But for my buddy and me he would have fallen on the steps.

"What's the trouble, Cousin Boyd?" I asked as my poor relative groaned and threatened to expel the contents of his stomach on the sidewalk.

"Swallowed my wad, son...swallowed my wad."

"How did that happen?" Sharkey wanted to know.

"It was that ol' Goodman lady — she done it."

"Swallowed your wad for you?"

"No, but she sure made me do it, though."

Not until we had promised to take him home and had draped him with the versatile burlap to prevent his vomiting on the seat of The Carcass did he explain: "Well, sir, I guess I must've been kinda dozing along — it was during that 'Revive Us Again' song — when all of sudden that old woman reached over and busted me. It must've been her, cause there wasn't anybody between her and me and there wasn't anybody behind me either. She was mad 'cause I made her give me my pew."

"Maybe you fell asleep and dropped your head against the back of your pew," I suggested.

"No, son, it was that ol' Goodman woman. When I looked at her she was grinnin' like a starved mule marooned on an island of prickly pears."

"What's the matter, boys?" The inquiry came from Mr. McKinney, who had been listening to the service from the vestibule and had noted our untimely exit.

"He swallowed his wad, Mr. McSkinney."

"Ever swallow your wad, Mr. McPenny?"

"Tobacco wad?"

Before either of us could answer, the sick one uncurled from a tattoo of gags long enough to say, "Mack, don't let anybody tell you that gosh dern old Goodman lady is a Christian! Just because I made her move out of my seat, she hit me so hard while I was asleep I swallowed a whole plug."

"That's sure too bad," the janitor sympathized.

To us he said, "I got something I sure need to talk about to you fellers."

"Now listen, Mack," fumed Cousin Boyd, "if it's about me spittin' on the auditorium floor, I can tell you I haven't done that since I got converted last revival time. Carry my spittoon with me now." At this point he pulled a small tin can from its place in the pocket with the brandy container and the little Bible.

"Nope, nope, it ain't that, Mr. McCord. It's got something to do about a feller that tried to...well, I'll talk to you boys about it later."

"We'll be back just as soon as we take Lefty's cousin home, Mr. McPenny."

Not long after Cousin Julia had assumed charge of her miserable husband and the canal had relieved us of his burlap napkin, we returned to keep my buddy's promise to Foxy Mack.

Had the latter found a forged letter we had scribbled to Jasper O. Rice and dropped intentionally on the furnace room floor? We would know very soon.

The janitor must have been watching for us, for we had hardly parked The Carcass in a vacant lot opposite the church when he bobbed up from the basement stairway and motioned us to join him.

"I always did figger I could count on you fellers, if I ever needed advice or hep of any kind."

"Your inference is not without genuine justification, Mr. McSkinney."

"Huh?"

"I said that you're right in your belief."

"Yep, yep, that's what I figger. So I'm gonna let you read what that cussed Rice feller must've lost. Found it on the floor."

With Mr. McKinney and Carl for an audience I read my disguised scribbling, which addressed *"Dear Jasper"* and which stated:

" `I was sure glad to get your invitation to come and live with you in that church attic. You are sure a smart guy and I'm sure proud to call you brother. Ma always said you was a good hustler. I am sure tired of *living in dump yards so I am going to come and take you up on that invite. Say, kid, don't throw any more water or anything on that dumb janitor cause he might get the preacher or a cop to find your hideout and put you in a cooler. But if he did stool on you and they caught you, it sure would make that janitor a silly guy not being able to catch you all the time you was living in the church. Well, you can sure expect me in sometime this week. Adiós, kid.*

Your bud,
Horace' "

"How do you suppose he gets in and out of the building, Mr. McSkinney?" I inquired, folding up the letter and placing it in my pocket.

"I ain't as dumb as that cussed joker thinks I am, boys. I examined the locks on the front doors and one of 'em is all scratched. He's been scraping the bolt with a knife."

"Good deduction, Mr. McPenny," put in Carl.

"What you think I oughta do, fellers?"

"Well, whatever you do, Mr. McSkinney, don't tell Brother Goodman or any of the local police. It's just as Jasper's brother suggested, you'd be the laughing stock of the town if somebody else had to be called in to oust a tramp who had been living in the church right under your very nose."

"Lefty's absolutely right," supported Sharkey. "Tell you what, Mr. McPenny: We'll wait until this Horace lad establishes residence with his brother and then the three of us will tickle their ribs with a gun and take the reprobates to a place where they'll be looking through bars instead of stained windows."

"Yes, and we'll give you all the credit, Mr. McSkinney."

"And the board of stewards will surely raise your salary for that sort of work, Mr. McPenny. Sound good?"

"Yep, yep. Sure does."

"Okay, Mr. McPenny, Saturday afternoon you get the building heated so we can do our duty comfortably that night, and we'll be by for you sometime between seven and eight o'clock. By Saturday Jasper's brother will have moved into the attic with his villainous brother, and we'll attend to both of them."

"I always did figger I could count on you fellers."

CHAPTER NINE

Threats From Bossy Betsy

Tuesday morning, two days later, the sun was just taking wing from the mountainous dome of Old Rusty when we paused en route to Professor Holdbolt's lecture room to scan the college bulletin board.

"See anything interesting, Lawrence?"

At first I did not understand the inquiry, for close by in a small cement pond, a noisy jet of water climbed vertically from the mouth of a weird iron gargoyle and splattered back on porous rocks that looked like human shoulders trying to come out of a perpetual rain.

"Not a thing, Carl," I said in answer to his repeated question, "unless... oh, but we've already got a date with Foxy Mack. Guess we'll just...."

"Are you alluding to the dance the toe-heads are giving the Zetas and the Psi Chis, my mischievous friend?"

"I am, indeed, oh thou of the telepathic brain."

"And you were, perchance, thinking that we might descend upon them as they slide over the Country Club floors, and that we might sneak into the basement and that there we might blow a fuse?"

"I was, indeed, telepathy personified. But I wonder if it wouldn't be better to save that sort of deed for some night when we don't have something else to attend to."

"Yeah, guess we'd better spare the brawlers this time and devote our full attention to Mr. McPenny. Now if...."

To determine the cause of Sharkey's discontinuation, I let my eyes follow his to Professor Holdbolt's multi-windowed classroom where Bossy Betsy, the professor's student secretary, was building a stack of Spanish test papers on a walnut desk.

"The ol' girl is getting ready to leave at last," observed my partner-to-be in the underhanded enterprise we had planned at 1:30 a.m., after much cramming for the Spanish examination scheduled for 9:00 a.m.

"Sharkey, a last, desperate alternative occurs to me: How about asking Betsy if she know the answers to the five questions we can't answer?"

"If she knew, she wouldn't tell us. And if we were to ask the wench about them and Prof, with his uncanny powers, later discovered that someone took from his exam lottery cage of 120 numbered marbles a certain unholy five bearing the numerals of the very questions we had asked Bossy about, we'd be suspects number one, sure as I'm a featherless Beebuzzard."

"Guess you're right. Well, I'm really glad Betsy is finally pulling out. I can think of a thousand things more pleasant than shivering outside this building as we've been doing for the past hour waiting for that red-topped shrew to get the heck out of Prof's lair."

"Patience, my good Nelson. And resort not to the vulgar slang of the proletariat, even in this hour of tribulation. Be of good cheer, for behold the damsel approachest en route to ye aulde canteen."

"Forgive mine tongue, Sir Carl, for the utterance of such vile speech. May it be purged with live coals that its future utterances may be acceptable unto thee."

"Good morning, Betsy."

"What in the world are you doing on the campus so early, Betsy?"

"Really, Lawrence, I can't see that's any of your concern."

"I'm sorry, I didn't mean to be so inquisitive. I was just curious."

"And what's the difference in being curious and inquisitive, I might ask?"

Was it the January breeze and the sound of precipitating water, or was it Betsy that sent a quiver along the seam of my vertebra?

"Now, Bossy...I mean Betsy...."

"What did you call me, Carl Lewis?"

"Why, *Betsy*, of course."

"I'm almost positive you said something else."

"It must have been that fountain that made it sound like something else."

"Well, whatever it was, I want to tell you two right now that in the presence of Professor Holtbolt's students you are going to call me `Miss Snerd.' Do you understand now?" I said `Miss Snerd,' not `Betsy.'"

"Pray tell me, your Royal Highness," queried Carl, "why have you assumed this starchy attitude? Are we but knaves that thou shouldst deny us the ecstasy that comes to us when we pronounce thy sweet name...the blessed name `Betsy'?"

"Stop trying to be funny, Carl. I'm serious now. I mean what I say."

"Now let me get this straight, Betsy," I put in. "I want to be sure the tympanic membrane in my auditory canal (biology study does have its advantages sometimes) didn't revise the sound you made in our direction. If I heard rightly, you just said a moment ago that we're to prefix the title `Miss' to your surname."

"Now aren't you two just too cute for words." Sarcasm wore long breeches on the young woman's face.

I seemed to have split the breeches when I reminded the coed that after all she and my buddy had graduated from high school together. "And, by the way, as I recall, Sharkey's name was listed on the honor roll of his class. Somehow I don't seem to recall that Supt. Johnson read *your* name, Betsy."

"Pull your punches, Left, or you'll have the poor girl squalling like a babe in an overripe diaper."

"You two are just as crude as ever, I see." Her lower lip dashed over a barricade of dental work and curled downward in an expression of disgust. "And since you seem to be in such a recalling mood, Lawrence, you might recall how Sharkey, as you call him, disgraced himself and our whole class by taking his diploma from Mr. Johnson and then shaking his hand with a big wad of chewing gum."

"I object, Your Honor!" I exclaimed, turning to the weird gargoyle as if it were a presiding judge. "I object on the grounds that the little incident of graduation night has no bearing on the present case. On behalf of my righteous client, I request that Miss Snerd's irrelevant reference be stricken from the records. Your Honor, did I hear you say, `Objection sustained and request granted'? Thank you, Your Honor, and remind me to buy you an umbrella sometime."

"Now aren't you just too cute for words."

"You said that before, Betsy," I reminded. "Remember? You're in a rut."

And Carl was quick to add: "Yeah...a muddy one, too."

"Now listen, you two, and let me explain, as I started to do a minute ago, why I want you to call me `Miss Snerd' instead of `Betsy.' It's just that I'm due that much respect since, after all, I am a college instructor's secretary!"

Carl's facial comma stood in alto-rilievo as he flung incisively, "My dear Miss Snooty, I dislike correcting you, but, since I am truly concerned with your welfare, I shall: My dear, an instructor is one of lesser rank than a professor. Your employer is a professor, not a lowly instructor."

And close upon the heels of my confederate's missile came mine: "Why be chesty about your little job, Betsy? As if any little freshman with the sense of a mosquito couldn't use a key as you do and grade the objective type of exams Prof gives."

"Well, that's not all I do."

"Say, Shark," said I, as if our third person were elsewhere, "they tell me that lots of college secretaries are paid according to the dexterity with which they mount their bosses' knees."

"Now you just listen to me! I'm not that kind! I'll have you know I keep my position as secretary to Professor Holdbolt purely on the merits of my good academic ability."

"Hurray for Snerd!" exclaimed Carl, jumping to the ledge of the cement encasement that encircled the fountain and pool.

"Did you hear that, Judge? `Ray for Betsy! Betsy for governor! No, Betsy for President!"

Joining the co-leader of the Royal Society of the Beebuzzards, I ascended the cement to address the 40,000 with: "My friends, it is my extreme honor and pleasure to present to you at this time the onery... I mean the honorable Miss Betsy Snooty, our choice for President of these United States!"

"Huzza!" shouted Carl above his loud clapping. "Huzza!"

"Who's a what!" I responded.

"Betsy's a snoot! Long live Betsy, our next chief executive!"

By this time, our candidate was building distance between herself and us.

Hardly more than a catcall away, however, she wheeled about and warned: "Carl Lewis, hereafter when you head your papers, you'd sure better follow instructions and stop abbreviating the month of the year."

"Just trying to save your pretty eyes for the moonlight, my dear. Did anyone ever tell you your eyes are like...."

"Just you violate instructions again and see if I don't count off 10 points. Professor Holdbolt has told me I may, if I like."

"You heard what the First Lady said, my quill comrade," I reminded Sharkey.

"And as for you," she said, turning her attention to me, "you don't have to henscratch just because you're left-handed. You'd better write plainer from now on, Mr. Lawrence Nelson."

"Did you hear that, Sharkey? She called me `Mister!' Hurray, I'm a man! Miss Snooty Snerd, alias `Bossy Betsy,' just made a man of me!"

Decending on one knee to the ground, my buddy extended a hand in childlike humility and begged, "Please, sir, give me a coin that I may feed my famished stomach with a loaf."

"Not one farthing, boy, until you have wiped the dust off my shoes and...."

It was useless to continue our act, for Bossy had already departed.

As she neared the canteen, Carl clapped his hands to his mouth and cried, "Betsy, the more I know you, the more I know why you didn't get that ex-man of yours to the altar!"

"Oh, well, I never did particularly care for A's," I muttered.

"Well, now that the ol' hen's left her roost, let's go into the coop and gather in the eggs."

"Lead on, Sir Carl."

The eggs were little black balls bearing numerals in white. We took all 120 of them from their nest, a global lottery cage of one-foot diameter supported on wooden framework by means of a steel axle terminating in a small crank designed to turn the globe and thereby release the marbles, whose numbers were to indicate to the class what questions they were to answer.

"Okay, Left, now look at the mimeographed sheets Prof gave us and call out the numbers opposite those cussed questions we can't answer."

We had just located the marbles under search when feminine heels clicked toward the scene of our clandestine project.

"Betsy?"

"I don't know, Lefty, but, for gosh shakes, let's slam these things back where we got them and pretend we're studying!"

In his haste, Carl missed the aperture in the globe and the marbles bounced on the floor.

The clicking came nearer and louder. But just at the moment when we expected Bossy to open the door and make her unwelcome reappearance, the heels passed on.

"The librarian," I breathed in relief.

"Left, let's leave the marbles on the floor and scram!"

Minutes later, we retired to the library to study and await the hour of the Spanish examination.

Would the freed marbles go unnoticed by Professor Holdbolt till after test time?

"Sharkey," said I, "maybe we ought to invoke the prayers of the 40,000 other Beebuzzards. When Prof finds those things...."

"Yeah," added Carl, "to use one of Foxy's adjectives, I'm 'scart' too! That man will know sure that we two are the culprits and our intent."

CHAPTER TEN

Action in the Classroom

At exactly 9:00 a.m. diminutive Professor Holdbolt, sawing his neck on a stiff collar and wagging a big brown satchel under the arm of a dingy blue serge coat fox-trotted into his Spanish classroom and glanced with characteristic self-consciousness at his 26 would-be linguists.

Although no one had ever proved why the man was never without his punishing high collar, there were those who had their theories. There were some, for instance, who would tell you that he wore the lofty fabric in order to stretch his neck and extend his meager height. Others would say that he wore it to hide a mole, which, according to rumor, had the appearance of a set of Ethiopian buttocks. Others insisted that his wife compelled him to wear it so that he would not be looking down at shapely knees protruding unshielded from front desks.

To cover up some of his self-consciousness, the professor was accustomed to fondle a yardstick while he lectured. Now that he was ready to address the class, he rapped the stick against the floor in a signal for quietude.

"Young ladies and young gentlemen," he began in a strong voice, another weapon he hoped would convince himself as well as others that he was calm and collected rather than ill at ease.

At this point he stopped and glared at a coed who was blowing her nose. Too late the latter remembered the temperamental and fastidious man's perpetual insistence on absolute silence while he spoke.

Embarrassed, she rooted her nose into a flimsy handkerchief and looked up with an expression that plainly pleaded for forgiveness.

There were occasions when Professor Holdbolt, who was proud of the almost incredible fact that he had been a sergeant in World War I, seemed to daydream that he was still on the drill field.

He must have been daydreaming now, for he roared the unfortunate girl down farther into her seat with: "Sound off, Adams! Sound off!"

The yardstick snapped to attention and rapped cadence with the third command: "Sound off, Adams!"

Obeying "Sergeant" Holdbolt's command, "Private" Joy Adams blew two weak blasts. And as she blew, an application of pink rouge on her face tiptoed into the background to let a bold blush further ornament her dimpled cheeks.

Satisfied that the disturbance had ended, Holdbolt dismissed his military bearing and said somewhat kindly, "Thank you, Miss Adams."

After twice drawing his neck bravely across the tall collar (we sometimes rather expected him to groan during such ordeals), he caressed the stick and began marching back and forth across the room. Some said the professor paced to relieve his nervousness, while others contended he paced to get a better view of female legs.

Addressing the entire group, he said, "Now then, young ladies and young gentlemen, I am prepared to allow you three minutes during which you may ask any questions you may have before we begin our examination."

Buster Turner (otherwise known as "Saber Fang," because of a crooked tooth), who not infrequently showed spurts of Beebuzzardism, winked at us and said to Professor Holdbolt, "Prof, what about that expression `hay'? Does it mean `there are' as well as `there is'?"

"Yes, señor Turner, it may take singular subjects or it may take plural."

"Then it's correct to say `Hay un perro allí,' meaning `There is a dog there.' " While he was inquiring, Buster pointed directly at the man in the high collar.

Professor Holdbolt's refusal to tolerate joking or impertinence in his classroom was well known among the class members and so, with three exceptions, the students remained respectfully silent. We three, however, indulged in a little snicker party that stopped only when Saber Fang's victim pointed three fingers in our direction and said unsmilingly, "Yes, señor Turner, and it is also correct to say, `Hay tres perros allí,' meaning `There are three dogs there.'"

After making a few other explanations, he of the tall neckpiece announced that "Miss Snerd will conduct the examination, as I have a pressing engagement in town." We learned later that the "pressing engagement" was an appointment with a tailor, none other than Cousin Boyd, whom he paid to pad the shoulders of his serge coat. "The young men," he told my blabbing relative, "are inclined to be more respectful to a man with big shoulders."

With a nod to Bossy Betsy, Professor Holdbolt reached for his satchel and was about to depart when he stepped on something that rolled one leg from under him and sent him sprawling awkwardly against Saber Fang, who, in an evident attempt to steady the man, jerked off a button from the blue serge; whether or not the youth intended to dismantle the garment is still a matter of debate among his classmates.

"Well, we can't be victorious all the time," whispered Carl as we watched the vexed one and his secretary align the marbles in chronological order to determine which ones were missing.

"He was too smart for us."

"Well, heck, Lefty, anybody could find a thing under his foot."

His voice booming, the professor instructed, "Young ladies and young gentlemen, you will write the answers to these five questions."

After reading the numbers of the miniature spheres we had removed from the lottery cage, he then gave us 15 more questions.

"And now, young ladies and young gentlemen, just before I leave you in Miss Snerd's charge, I wish to offer a twenty-dollar reward for information leading to the conviction of the person or persons who took some marbles from our revolving globe."

"I've got an idea, Sharkey," I whispered, beckoning my buddy to follow me.

We overtook him in the corridor.

"Professor Holdbolt, we'd like a word with you," said I.

"All right, señor Lewis."

"Sir, you have confused our names again."

"To be sure. I beg your forgiveness. It's because you seem to be together so much."

"It's nothing, sir. Sir, we have a clue to report." I knew he'd like that military approach. Three cheers for R.O.T.C. training!

"Let's have it, then, Pri...I mean señor Nelson."

"Well, sir, about 10 minutes before the 9 o'clock bell, we happened to pass back to Haven Hall."

"Yes?"

"Back of Haven Hall, we saw a fellow on his knees and thumbing something along the ground. When we got closer, he looked up at us and said, `How about playing some marbles with me?'"

"Lawrence and I just happened to remember," contributed Carl, "those marbles were just about the size of yours."

"Well, who was this chap?"

"His name, sir, is Rice...Jasper O. Rice. Isn't that right, Carl?"

"Absolutely! We felt it our duty to report our observation, because we certainly didn't want you to suspect that any of your students would stoop to such a shameful felony. We would all feel extremely hurt if you distrusted any of us."

"Be assured, young gentlemen, that I did not for a single moment entertain the idea that any of you were guilty. I have the utmost confidence in all members of my classes."

"Thank you, sir. We appreciate your trust in us."

"Now then...about the guilty one. Is he a freshman?"

"No, sir."

"Sophomore?"

"No, sir."

"Junior?"

"No, sir."

"I see. Merely because he is a senior, he presumes that he can pursue whatever course suits his fancy. I'm afraid that too often the senior takes advantage of the fact that he...."

"But, sir, he isn't...."

"Now, young man, on other occasions you have taken issue with me on some other matters of opinion. Now in this case, don't you think that my experience and age make me better qualified than you to know seniors?"

"Yes, sir."

"Prof, Lawrence was only trying to tell you that Jasper O. Rice is not enrolled at Yucca College — and that he did, at least, return the marbles, in a way, by going back and flinging them floorward!"

"Not one of our students?"

"No, sir."

"Well, why didn't you...I'm sorry I became a trifle irritated, señor Nelson."

Again he begged my forgiveness; again I reassured: "It's nothing, sir."

If the professor's suspicions were ever to be aroused, surely they must have been aroused when Carl and I began conflicting descriptions of the suspect. We were both overly eager to describe him and unfortunately Sharkey started giving him our number one version, the same he had handed out to Foxy Mack, and I began with version number two, the same we had given Alice. We were quick, however, to come to an agreement, and Carl explained that he had been about to describe Jasper O. Rice Senior.

Apparently convinced that Jasper was beyond jurisdiction of college authorities, Professor Holdbolt seemed far less inclined to bring him to justice. Assured that the boy was not a frequent visitor on the campus, he conveniently forgot the reward he had offered.

Bossy Betsy met our return to the classroom with a frown.

"What makes you two think you can leave this room without my permission?" she demanded.

"We had urgent business with Prof," I answered in a low voice, hoping we might make our conversation private.

But Betsy, confident that she had us in an embarrassing situation, craved an audience.

"And how do I know you didn't go out and look in your books for answers to the exam questions you were assigned?"

"We left our papers and books here, Miss Snerd" was Sharkey's reply.

"Johnny," said the redhead to one of her favorites, a 185-pound halfback, "I want you to search these two and see if they have any answers to the exam questions."

"I'd rather not, Betsy."

"Now, Johnny, don't be disrespectful," said I. "Remember it's 'Miss Snerd,' not 'Betsy.' The lady just told us a couple of hours ago not to call her by her first name."

"When I want a comment from you, Lawrence, I'll ask for it," snapped Bossy. "Now then, Johnny, you are going to turn these two's pockets wrong side out. Hurry, Johnny, so we can get back to work!"

"Well, orders is orders, pal."

"Hurry up, Johnny," urged the presiding secretary.

"You sure you want me to do this, Bet?"

"I'm positive. Now go ahead. Do you hear me?"

"Remember what I told you, Johnny," warned my fellow Beebuzzard.

"Too bad, Lewis, but when I set out to do a thing I don't let my chili come up."

No chili did come up, but Sharkey's fist did. It was a quick right uppercut that converted the halfback's chin into a sort of small human Ferris wheel.

His soiled handkerchief wet with saliva, Saber Fang mopped the white face of the horizontal athlete while frantic Betsy rubbed his wrist and ordered her excited class members back to their seats. Eventually her wide eyes looked accusingly at the puncher.

"Carl," she railed, "I knew you were low, but I didn't know you were this low!"

"Seems to me like Johnny is the one who's low" was Saber Fang's remark. But when Betsy focused her wrath on him, he explained quickly, "Now that was just a pun. What I really meant was that Johnny is stretched out low on the floor."

A medley of moans from the fallen gridster as he rallied and blinked to consciousness was followed with his inevitable question: "What happened?"

"You were going to search a guy who didn't want to be searched," said Fang.

"Don't you worry, Johnny," Betsy consoled, "he never could have beaten you in a fair fight. I'm going to tell Dean Hargrove all about it, and Mr. Carl Lewis will more than likely be expelled, and it'll serve him right! He and that sidekick of his don't ever do anything but cause trouble."

"You know," I said to my buddy an hour or so later, as we passed the pond and saw the weird gargoyle sticking his tongue of water out at us, "I'm afraid this Jasper lad is going to get us into trouble one of these days."

CHAPTER ELEVEN

Foxy Without a Light Again

Came Saturday night, the time for our date with Foxy Mack.

Treading over a wintry wind-swept road of gravel and grains of sand, which I ground between my teeth until they took refuge in a pair of young cavities, I arrived at the Lewis home. It was an aged adobe structure with banging doors that seemed to be playing cops and robbers with the rough gale.

"Lawrence, better have some boiled eggs and steak with us," invited Carl's older brother as he pointed to a chair and raked a napkin across his chin to remove a bit of yellow yolk.

"Thanks, Arthur, but I just had supper."

"In that case, you won't be able to join us in some rice pudding with whipped cream," remarked Carl. "Too bad, Left." How well he knew that his mother's rice pudding was one of my favorite desserts.

"Are you sure you wouldn't like just a little pudding, Lawrence?" asked Mrs. Lewis.

"Well, I...."

"Mother, didn't you hear him say he's already eaten?"

Confound Carl! He knew that my gustatory organs were almost crying out for a fling at that pudding.

"I know but he always seem to like...."

"Now, mother, Lawrence and I are in training. The college boxing tournament comes off next month, and you certainly don't want him to overindulge in sweets and be eliminated. Lefty's going after the lightweight title, and I'm trying for the welterweight." How very thoughtful of Carl!

"Oh, then, I'm so sorry I tempted him."

"That's all right, Mrs. Lewis. But as a matter of fact, I didn't..."

"Don't worry, mother, you didn't tempt Lefty. He's got too much will power to break training. Man of indomitable will...that's Lefty." I was hoping prayerfully that Carl would be strangled by the heaping spoonful of pastry he was now elevating to his eager palate.

I waited until his mouth was packed beyond speakability and then I burst forth to his parent with: "As a matter of fact. Mrs. Lewis, we didn't have any dessert at the house tonight."

I almost bit my lips in hoggish eagerness as Mrs. Lewis handed me a bowl of pudding topped by a tall cone of whipped cream which threatened to avalanche into a valley of puffed rice and raisins.

"Poor old dad's going to feel slighted when he finally comes in from the cow barn and finds there isn't any more pudding," said Sharkey.

"Well, in that case," I responded, pushing back my bowl and swallowing a mouthful of lonely saliva, "we'd better leave this for him."

Sharkey shrieked in merriment, patted me on the shoulder, and shoved the enticing pastry back to me.

"Guy," he chuckled, "we've got enough pudding in the ice box to supply an army. I just wanted to make your mouth drip. Dive in, boy!"

Great fellow — my pal Sharkey. I'd fight for him, but, by thunder, I'd have to retaliate for the misery he had caused me at the table tonight. Just wait...I'd have my fun one of these nights when he was a visitor at the Nelson shack.

"What do you boys have planned for the evening?" inquired Mrs. Lewis when our stuffed pouches eventually won their appeals for mercy.

"Oh, we've got obligations at the church, Mrs. Lewis."

"Well, I'm so glad you boys have something like that to take up your spare time. Lots of young people are getting caught in all sorts of mischief these days simply because they've nothing worth while to do."

"Well, you needn't worry about our getting caught in mischief, Mrs. Lewis."

"Guess we'd better be rattlin' along, Left."

"Yes, we wouldn't want affairs held up because we were late."

"No, always set a good example for the others," put in the admonishing mother.

"Mean night," observed Carl as we squeaked-opened the doors that sheltered The Carcass in a casket of aging metal.

If I ever wondered how elevated a child feels in his high chair, the lofty seat of the Model T put my wondering to rest.

I was trying to slam my door shut when suddenly I shot upward.

"What in the name of common sense is wrong, Lefty?"

"As if you didn't know!"

I was still holding the door handle and running my hand along the thin upholster where my rump had been when I got another jolting.

My anger at being shocked twice by what I recognized to be one of Sharkey's latest electric devices, which the inventor obviously controlled with a button attached to his steering rod, was dispelled by his explanation: "I hooked it up to try out Mr. McPenny's reflexes tonight."

The janitor must have been waiting our arrival, for one weak belch from The Carcass' hoarse horn brought him fox-trotting like a henpecked husband sneaking out to a burlesque show.

"You look mighty spry tonight, Mr. McPenny," complimented Carl as he thumbed the button on the steering rod and watched he of the eagle beak ram his head into the top of the coupe.

"Easy, Mr. McSkinny! What's the trouble?"

The Beebuzzards managed to hold serious faces, even when their bewildered victim began rubbing his hams and insisting he had sat down on a bumblebee at large in his trousers.

"Giving yourself a birthday spanking, Mr. McPenny?"

"Nope, nope, just tryin' to murder that cussed insect."

Satisfied that he had killed the offender, Foxy Mack eased down again and made another attempt to close the door.

This time Carl gave the button three short jabs and Foxy hunched as many times, as if he were trying to get in step at a conga line.

"Fellers," he concluded at length, "that's a shock I'm gittin.' I got it that time in the hand and the other place too. Ain't no bee that can git outa my breeches and light on my hand that fast."

If the man suspected that somehow with deliberate design we were responsible for his electrical shake-up, my buddy evidently put his suspicions to bed by saying, "The wires on this wreck are getting rotten. That's the second short circuit I've found in the last hour."

At the church, Mack's ever protuberant eyeballs stepped another degree forward when Sharkey pulled a .22 calibre pump from the floor of the The Carcass and said, "By golly, this little persuader ought to make Jasper and his bud get in high."

"But, fellers, we sure don't aim to kill them fellers, do we?"

"Maybe not, Mr. McSkinny, but, after all, if we did, we might save ourselves a lot of trouble."

"Now, fellers, let's stop and talk this thing out. If we was to shoot one of them jokers up there in the attic, we'd have the law on us sure. Fellers, now I got a family and...."

"Aw, stop your worrying, Mr. McSkinny. If we shoot, we'll try to do nothing more than merely shoot their pegs from under them."

"I know, fellers, but you can't always hit a man where you want to...specially in the dark."

"True, true, Mr. McPenny," conceded Carl. "But suppose we did misaim and a fatality occurred. We could easily destroy the body in the furnace, and no one but us three would ever miss them. After all,

Jasper doesn't seem to have any folks other than his brother. And if we got him, too, then...."

"Fellers, now I used to do a little cussin'...`fore I got myself this church job, you understand...and I have been knowed to take a little snort or two on New Year's and the Fourth, but, fellers, I sure ain' never took part in a killin' and...."

"Mr. McSkinny, you seem to have forgotten that we came down here tonight just to help you in a matter that's really no concern of ours. Don't you appreciate our interest in your welfare?"

"Yep, yep."

"Then where's your spirit of cooperation?" Carl's customary appeal to Mack on the grounds that he was the guardian of the church and its natural protector whose Christian duty it was to make the transgressor pay even the supreme price if need be met with defeat, and finally the man threatened to go home unless we agreed to let him carry the rifle.

"If I tote the gun," he explained, "nobody's gonna git killed, `cause I sure ain' gonna do nothing else more than bluff with it."

Too bad that Carl had gone to the expense of buying a box of blanks, I thought, as I watched the janitor assume temporary possession of the .22. We would have had great sport feeling him shake while we pretended to send non-existing bullets into a pair of non-existing bodies. But the night was young; perhaps we would yet take charge of the gun.

"Hope you didn't forget to heat the place up, Mr. McSkinny."

"I got the whole place all steamed up like we was gonna have regular preachin'."

"I'll hold your flashlight for you," said Carl to the droopy-eared one as the latter searched for the key hole at the main entrance. After the lock had assumed a Sunday position, my buddy snapped off the flashlight beam and said, "There are certain precautions we'd better take. In the first place, we'd better keep our lights off until we catch our men. We can feel our way along and keep together by holding hands, and, of course, you'll have one hand busy with the gun, Mr. Mack, and so I'll just hold on to your arm and you can let Lefty have your other paw. Now in the second place, we'd better continue to whisper just as we are doing now."

Inside we halted again in the blackness and voiced our plan of attack until my buddy had sufficient time in which to loosen Foxy's bulb as he had done on another occasion. At last he returned the flashlight to its owner and we groped down the main aisle, Sharkey in the lead, Foxy pinned in the middle, and I bringing up the rear.

To an outsider having the nocturnal seeing ability of a cat we would have presented a queer spectacle, a weird pageant in which two youths and a shaggy-haired man carrying a gun crept stealthily toward a holy altar as if they were besieging a demon who had taken refuge there. How absurd — absurd as a polar bear drinking hot chocolate in a Turkish bath!

Leaving the auditorium, we made our way through a narrow corridor to the foot of a corkscrew stairway. There in the dusty light that leaked weakly through a quartet of stained panes, we stopped to whittle on Mr. McKinney's nerves.

"Now you fellows remember," gulped my buddy in counterfeit fear, "that if anything tragic happens...say two of us are laid out by these rascals, then the thing for the third guy to do is to escape and bring a doctor and maybe an ambulance."

"What about a cop, fellers?"

"Mr. McPenny, you've got to understand the cops are the last people we want to call in on this case. Sabe?"

"Yep, yep."

As we made our slow ascent up the steps, the old boards that my grandmother had once trod en route to her kindergarten classes popped creakingly. And to further prepare Foxy Mack for the frightened condition we hoped would finally overpower him, I swallowed audibly and let my hand tremble slightly in his.

When we were halfway up, Sharkey secretly flipped a rock to the floor above and we stopped motionless as if we'd fallen into an ice mold. After a full minute, our leader tugged us forward and assured, "Just a rat."

"Yep, but does it have two legs?" quivered Foxy.

I gave him another dose of swallowing and trembling, and Sharkey did his bit by reminding us to keep low, "lest Jasper make us his ducks in an improvised shooting gallery."

Another stone, another halting, and then the suggestion: "Fellers, these fellers ain' really doing no harm up there. Maybe we'd oughta leave 'em be."

"Why, Mr. McSkinny," said I, "I'm astonished! Are you losing your religion, your reason, your self-respect? Didn't Jasper sprinkle you with acid? Didn't he send Brother Goodman a crow...or something like that...and attach your name as the sender?"

"Yep, yep."

We weren't ready yet for him to race back down the stairway, and so we tightened our holds and half dragged him onward into the fear-inducing unknown.

If the basement counted as one story, we were four stories high when we reached the attic entrance, which consisted of seven steps ending in an upright door. There we stopped again.

"They don't have a light, or we could see it peeping from under the door crack" was my suggestion. "They're either not in or they've gone to bed."

"They've gone to bed," contributed Carl. "After all, there isn't any heat way up here, so you can bet those guys hit the hay early."

"Now then, Mr. Mack," said Carl, "I'm going to let the door swing open and then Lefty and I'll ease in and let you bring up the rear with your flashlight. When we've advanced a few feet inside, I'll give a low whistle and that's your signal to snap your switch and run a beam hurriedly around the whole place. When you locate the culprits, keep a beam in their faces and Lefty and I'll do the rest."

"I always did figger I could count on you fellers."

The three of us went down on our knees, the rusty hinges hummed, and we began crawling into a habitation of dust and musty odors.

Sharkey, his mouth yearning to roar into laughter, finally pursed his twitching lips together in the darkness long enough to emit that low whistle.

Clicks and snaps and an expression of anger from Foxy.

"Quick, turn on your light, Mr. McSkinny!"

"I heard something in the north corner, Mr. McPenny! Shine it on 'em! For gosh sakes, get the lead out!"

While the janitor snapped in vain and muttered bywords, we quietly changed locations in preparation to assume the roles of the Rice brothers.

And then it happened! A booming voice from the door wheeled our bewildered faces into a light so powerful that we were unable to see beyond it.

"I got a gun on you guys," the voice avowed. "Now put ya feelers up, like ya was reaching for the stars. And you in the dunce cap, hand me that rifle, 'fore ya let it go off and put somebody's eye out. Whadda ya guys doing in my playhouse, anyway?"

As the newcomer came nearer and snatched up the .22 from its bearer, we could see the vast difference in the two men's heights. The former was very tall; but his other features lingered concealed back in the night.

Since we Beebuzzards were apparently still too dismayed to respond, the third member of our trio offered a reply.

"Well, we was jist up lookin' to maybe clean up a little," he whimpered.

"Now ain't that interesting. And didja stop to think ya might get cleaned up yourself? Huh?"

Silence.

"I asked ya a question, Shorty. Didja hear me?"

"Yep, yep."

"Maybe I oughta try ya little pop gun on you guys...teach ya to be meddlin' 'round where ya ain't got no business."

"Now please, feller, we didn't mean no harm." Ordinarily Mack's whimpering would have bowled us over with snickers, but right now we somehow found snickers unappetizing.

"Yep, that's what I'm gonna do — drill all three of ya and leave ya up here for the rats to gnaw on. But I ain't gonna do it right now. Say, Shorty, you got a key to this door?"

"Yep, yep."

"Kin ya make good coffee, Shorty?"

"Yep, yep, sure can."

"Okay then. Get out ya key and I'm gonna lock these two guys up, and then you'n me are going down to the kitchen, and you're gonna make some coffee that sure better be good. And when my bud gets here, all you guys are gonna get it right in the neck...or maybe somewheres else."

The big one's hoarse laughter was diminished when the door was closed.

We heard the key turn in the lock and then retreating footsteps.

Carl was the first to speak.

"Lefty," he mused in disgust, "when we gave McKinney his nickname, we really picked the appropriate one."

"How right you are. But, by golly, I never thought I'd see that day when Foxy and a partner would pull a masterpiece as they did tonight. Did you?"

"Too bad his partner had to ruin it by mentioning his bud. I knew then that he was trying to impersonate Horace. Before that, I rather thought it might have been that some tramp was actually staying up here."

"Foxy really won this round."

"Don't be pessimistic, Lefty. The night's not over yet, you know."

CHAPTER TWELVE

Sprinting in the Dark

With our flashlights we explored our surroundings for an avenue of escape, but found none. We were in a prison of wood and sheet metal, a gloomy storage chamber of junk, except for a huge bell. Plastered with dust by the trowel of Time, the forgotten vessel of bronze and copper hung forlorn yet lordly in an indoor belfry which, evidently, had been on the outside at one time, probably before that last two stories were added to the edifice.

"Look at that thing, Carl," said I pensively. "Wonder how many people that big bulb has beckoned to services. Wonder how many bereaved ones it's summoned to the last rites of loved ones."

"Lefty, how can you be sentimental in a situation like this?"

"Sharkey, did you know about this bell's being up here?"

"No."

"Nor did I."

We stood there for a moment silently studying the bell in the combined rays of our two flashlights.

"How many people do you suppose know there's a belfry and a bell up here, Lawrence?"

"Maybe a few old-timers too old to hear it even if...say, guy, an idea just hit me in the head!"

"Lad, I know what it is, but let's don't ring that thing tonight, for gosh sakes!"

"Why not, Sharkey? Boy, that would really put Foxy on the spot."

"How?"

"Well, don't you see that he'd be afraid Brother Goodman or someone would beat it over here to investigate and find us up here locked in by this friend of his? There'd be some kind of cross examination that you can bet Foxy wouldn't like to be in. Right?"

"Yes, but we wouldn't enjoy being in it either, would we?"

"Guess it wasn't much of an idea, after all."

"A good idea, Lefty, but not for tonight. You know, I just happened to remember something that that old Negro, Jake Williams, the janitor here before Mack, said."

"The Jake who stays in Mr. Steven's servant house in the next block?"

"Uh huh. Old Jake said he quit his job here because the place was haunted. Now what would Jake think if he heard this thing clanging away on some quiet midnight? I bet he'd root a coupla slats out of his bed trying to get under it."

"What about the people who live next door and those across the street? They wouldn't be scared as Jake, but they'd do some running to their windows."

"Yes, and when they saw the entire building in darkness and remembered it, apparently, didn't have a belfry, boy, there'd be some telephoning of some kind."

Our joviality ceased when Carl began sniffing. "I smell something," he said.

At the door he bent low, placed his nose to the rather wide crack just above the sill, and, after a deep inhalation, said, "Coffee, Lefty, they're really making coffee down there, just as the big lad said they would."

If an odor could climb all the way from the basement, why couldn't the sound of the pair's voices? We cupped our ears, listened intently, and heard weak mumbling and a distant laugh.

Abruptly I wondered if we could fashion a key from a piece of wire that lay in one of the junk piles nearby.

I bent a small section into the desired shape and inserted it into the lock, but an obstruction within made its journey entirely too short.

"It must be...yes, it is, Lefty. Those guys left the key in the lock!"

"Why all the joy, my good Beebuzzard without the `Bee'? After all, the key is on the outside, out of our reach."

"Not for long...I hope, my perfumed chum from Polecat Gutter. A little artifice I learned from a Saturday night Western may do the trick and set us free. Ah, Freedom, thou luscious flake from paradise so dear to the soul of every Beebuzzard! Give me thy lips that I may press them until mine own do drip with nectar and cleanse mine hairy chest of reeking 'possum blood!"

"Forsooth, Sir Carl, such hot words! Methinks they fain would melt the asbestos girdle of Satan and cause a walrus' tusks to curl like candles on a griddle."

Securing a piece of roofing paper from another mound of rubbish, Carl chuckled, "Yep, yep, as Foxy would say, when I was ten I saw a movie in which the shoot-'em-up hero named Buckskin Joe pulled this one in order to escape from a cabin where some desperados had penned him in and applied a torch to keep his feet warm, I guess."

As he talked, my buddy attempted to slide the wrinkled roofing paper under the door.

"What did Buckskin Joe do when he got out?" I asked. "Did he lasso the dirty dozen, hog tie them, and then turn them over to the marshall?"

"Yes, but not before he had galloped his trusty pinto full speed ahead without a single stop until he had overtaken the bandits some eight miles beyond and had shot nine of the rascals' wrists without reloading his six-shooter."

"Three cheers for Buckskin!"

"And three cheers for this sheet of roofing!" It had slipped under now, and Carl, retaining an inch of it on our side, was now trying, by means of the wire, to shove out the key so that it would alight on the paper outside.

"Let's jar the lock," said I, grasping the doorknob and shaking the door.

A peal of laughter reached us.

"They think we're trying to knock the door down," smirked Sharkey.

The key still remained unmovable.

More bangings, more laughter from below, and more pushing with the wire. Then finally our cries of triumph as the key plunked on the floor.

And now we moved the precious bit of metal toward us by pulling its carrier, the roofing. Hugged up at last against the wooden barrier that was also our barrier, it stopped.

I was grunting my disappointment when Carl jerked the rest of the paper from under the door and hooked the object of our work with his wire.

"Hallelujah!" he exclaimed as he held it up for me to examine, as if I might have doubted its genuineness.

Before we began our quiet descent to the kitchen, we held a council of war. Our next movements planned, we started down the steps. At the foot of the second flight, we stopped to listen to a new noise. It sounded like a squeaking hinge.

Mr. McKinney must have been in the kitchen threshold, for we had no difficulty in understanding his speech. "I sure do thank you, Clem," he said, "for helpin' me put one over on them fellers. I'll give you a light to the street, and then I'm gonna come back to them jokers in the loft and give 'em a long tale 'bout you gittin' scart and hightailing it out with the key. Yep, and then I'll make 'em wait a coupla more hours up there while I make out like I've gone after a skeleton key."

"Ya sure you'll be able to handle everything now by yaself, Uncle Loyd?"

"Yep, yep. No use for you to stay and lose some sleep, Clem; you got a long ride back to the farm. I'll make out all right."

A raucous laugh came from the nephew. "You're gittin' a big kick outa makin' monkeys of them guys, ain't ya, Uncle Loyd?"

"Yep, yep. And them jokers needed a good lesson. And I'm just the man that kin do it."

"Ya dern tootin' ya are. And ya can sure make it look snazzy and real. I guess ya musta inherited some of ya old man's vaudeville ability."

"You sure did some good actin' yourself up there in that loft, boy. Reckon you, too, got some of papa's knack for actin'."

Whereas I may have become lately the chief premeditator in the Beebuzzard clan, Carl was, as ever, our emergency man whose quick brain took complete charge of our affairs whenever our previously devised plans needed immediate change or revision, as they did now. We had counted on creeping upon the two in the kitchen and...but why take time to mention what could not now come to pass?

"Come on, guy," directed my companion. "Back to the attic!"

In our ex-jail again we listened to Mack's cracking climb up the last flight of the stair to "them jokers in the loft." And then, on a signal from Carl, we rammed ourselves with grunts and yells against the door, pretending we were trying to force our way out.

After the fifth onslaught, Carl turned the knob and we burst out into the corridor, where we were instantly enveloped in a flashlight beam.

"That you, Mr. McSkinny?"

"Yep." The single "yep" was not the only revelation of Foxy's surprise; he had waited unnaturally long to answer, and his monosyllable had been a frail one.

"Fellers," he said when he had regained his composure, "I jist this minute got the best of that Rice feller. I got your gun back while the scamp was pourin' himself some coffee."

"Well, where is he? Did you knock him out, Mr. McPenny?"

"Nope, nope. His chin was too doggone high. But I sure made him run with this here firearm. I guess he's gone from here, fellers."

The janitor wanted to turn on the ceiling lights, but we insisted that we keep the building in darkness.

"Well, he might still be in the place somewhere" was Sharkey's explanation. "Tell you what, Lefty. You take the basement and the next floor, and Mr. McPenny and I'll search the two upper floors."

"Right!" I was going to have an opportunity to put my original plan into fulfillment after all.

For Act III of tonight's drama, we needed some stage property, and so on my way down I stopped by the storeroom and secured a pair of garbage cans, a mass of discard curtains, and some old newspapers.

In the kitchen I distributed the paper and the curtains equally in the cans, which I placed behind the big range. Next I lit the contents with a match and stood back for an observation.

When the flames bit into the cotton and began to dispense a duet of dissipated smoke columns, I climbed upon a table and unscrewed the kitchen globe.

The stage was almost set. Soon I would call the players.

Now while the place was becoming packed with smoke, I hurried to the storeroom for another bundle of curtains.

On the way back, I yelled frightfully, "Help! The kitchen's on fire! Sharkey, help! The kitchen's on fire, Mr. McSkinny! The kitchen's on fire!"

I had reiterated that the kitchen was on fire for a purpose, and now as Foxy stumbled frantically down from the third floor I hoped he would remember the coffee party in the kitchen and would think that he and his relative had let a hot coal fall unnoticed from the old stove.

Rollicking jubilantly upon the heels of the janitor came snickering Sharkey. He had heard our victim wail, "Oh, Lord, for God's sake, don't let her burn down!"

From behind a banister, I watched the man as he tumbled in an awkward hop, like a seasick kangaroo on roller skates, down the last flight of the stairway. "Lord," he moaned, "if you jist won't let her burn, I won't never do no cussin' again!"

"We've got to have help from the fire department!" I told him, desperation in my voice. "You or Jasper one must have gotten careless with the stove!"

"Aw, it was Jasper! Yep, it was Jasper!" Foxy vowed as he flipped the black button on the wall and got no response.

He stood coughing and praying in the smoky doorway, his bulging orbs swinging back and forth as he watched blossoms of scarlet flames lick upward from their containing basins, now invisible because of the darkness and smoke.

"I'll get a hose from the storeroom!" yelled Sharkey. "Lefty, you get to work with a dish pan! And you, Mr. McPenny, get the lead out and go get the fire department!" His final instruction — "Don't waste time trying to get to a telephone, but run to the station yourself!" — was an excellent one, for it would provide us Beebuzzard with more time in which to prepare for the janitor's return.

"Poor man," I remarked as I watched the retreating one collide with a coat hanger. "He's really tearing up the floor. And he's scared. Bet he needs a change of flannels already."

How sweet and considerate of Carl to yell this assurance: "Don't worry Mr. McKinney?" In this hour of tribulation for Foxy, Carl showed his kindness by actually addressing the man by his right name and saying, "We'll be doing our dernest here while you're gone!"

And Foxy stopped appealing to the Lord long enough to reply, "I always did figger I could count on you fellers!"

After we had reunited the light globe with its socket, Sharkey opened the windows in the kitchen and the hall and with a towel helped the ceiling fans expel the smoke, while I extinguished the fires in the cans and returned them to the storeroom.

With a moment to spare, we shoveled out the coals from the range and threw them in the furnace.

When the fire chief's siren died in the street outside, we were snuggled in a closet opposite the pantry. Here we would be nicely situated to enjoy the grand finale.

We heard perturbed Mack snapping switches to flood the church with illumination as he led the way to the fire.

"This way, Chief Wilkins!" he directed. "Hurry, feller, hurry!"

"What's this," I snickered to my buddy, "a one-man fire department?"

"Fear not, Saint Lawrence," said Carl, "the others will soon follow. This is a volunteer company, you know; you can't expect the other men to stay at the station for a measly 100 dollars a year."

Even as he spoke another siren whined on Main Street and a big engine chugged its conceit and stuck its red chest out, proud that it was going to church.

At last they burst into the kitchen — the two of them, Foxy and Chief Wilkins.

From our little crack we could see the former just standing there and focusing his flashlight on the spot where a few minutes ago he had seen those fierce flames.

The chief located a switch and the stage became cozy with illumination.

"Where's the fire, McKinney?"

"Look at poor old Foxy, Lawrence."

"What the heck's the matter with you, Pop? Where's the fire?"

The tall fireman had his fire extinguisher poised for action.

Now that the second siren outside had directed the populace of Mesa to its destination, it hummed, it purred, it murmured, and went back to its dreams.

"If this is your idea of a nice gag, fella, you...."

"But, Mister Chief, I tell you the fire was right here!"

In his desperation Foxy began to call us: "Fellers! Say, fellers! Where are you, fellers?"

He heard only an unintelligible cry from outside, the squeak of car brakes, a banging on the side door, and finally a fireman's question from the main auditorium: "Where is it, Chief!"

"Here I am, Joe," the chief called back. To McKinney he said, "Pop, you said there was a fire down here. Okay, then where was it?"

"It was going right up them walls."

"Them solid brick walls, Pop?"

"Yep, yep...well, at least...."

"Now look, fella, at least I've got a little sense, so don't try and make me swallow so much all at once. See?"

"Yep, yep."

"Now, let's see we were...come on in here, Joe! Here I am!"

The fire chief was dramatic enough to want an audience, and so he waited a brief moment until hose-bearing Joe and his assistant could be present for further developments.

Garbed in protective hats and long coats, the two puffing newcomers had their questions along with their hose, but their superior silenced them with a twist of the wrist.

"I'll do the talking," he announced. "Men, this ol' guy here drags us all down here at bedtime and tells us there was a fire crawling up them brick walls. Either one of you fellas ever see brick burn?"

"Well, maybe it jist looked like them flames was climbing up the brick," defended Mack.

"Well, Pop, you better get yourself some glasses. And next time you think you see a fire and you feel like calling the department, first go over and sit down on it. And if it takes your pants and makes a big red-hot doughnut out of your end zone, give us a ring."

Laughter. The appearance of another fireman. An instant of quietude when we heard the voices of fire fans from the sidewalk. And then more footsteps in the hall.

"But, I tell you, fellers, there was flames over there somewhere. We made some coffee right here in this stove jist a little while ago and I reckon we must've jist sorta let a few fall out. This here old...."

"There ain't any coals in here, Pop." The chief had lifted a lid and peered in. "Maybe you jest took a little snooze and had a dream."

More laughter.

"Nope, nope, I don't sleep none, 'cept at home in my bed. You fellers trying' to be funny, and you ain't."

"Now you hadn't oughta said that, McKinney." As he spoke, the chief collared Foxy and pulled him up into his own stratosphere so that trembling Mack was left supporting himself on his toes. "Now you come running to us and say you got a fire down here, and when we git here you ain't got one. And next you tell us the flames was tearing up a brick wall. You ain't satisfied with that, though. You gotta tell us you made some coffee on this wood stove, and there ain't no coals in the thing. And one more thing. When we first come down here, you looked around and started hollering, "Fellas, fellas!" — like there was somebody else down here."

"See if he's got whiskey on his breath, Chief." This from Joe.

"Okay, McKinney, open your mouth and breathe out hard."

The short one started to obey, became confused and emitted a short snort instead.

"I said blow your breath, Pop, not your nose." And after a few whiffs from Foxy, the big man said, "No, nothing but a bad case of halitosis."

"Maybe that bad halitosis made him delirious," said a late arrival.

"He's just daffy," another contributed.

They were having their sport. Evidently they knew how to punish false alarmists. Maybe the Beebuzzard Society ought to issue bids to these lads.

"Chief, don't you think," said Joe, "we'd better turn 'im over to the bug house?"

"The next time something like this happens," said Wilkins, "we're gonna haft to send you somewhere, Pop. There're institutions for people that do things like this...and it ain't jail."

Why hadn't our victim told the entire story of events leading up to the false alarm? Maybe he feared that it would have met disbelief. Or perhaps he was afraid we might plan an even more extreme revenge. Or maybe he preferred to wait and give Brother Goodman a full account.

When all members of the comedy cast had gone, we crawled out of our close quarters. Carl stretched out on the table and I on a trio of chairs and we gave vent to unrestrained merriment.

And when our contortions were over, we agreed that we had not laughed so much in this kitchen since the night we sneaked in just before a cake walk, while some others were enjoying a song session, and iced Bossy Betsy's divinity loaf with cleansing cream.

CHAPTER THIRTEEN

Pie a La Commode

The second month of spring. The usual sand tonnage honeymooning with the ravishing wind and making greater champions of the local Liars Club, alias Mesa's Chamber of Commerce.

Since it was Good Friday and a holiday, we had resolved to do a good deed.

"Sharkey, I know just the thing we ought to do." We were in the living room of my house, where my buddy had been entertaining my hyperactive three year-old-sister Helen by drawing my picture on a toy blackboard. Helen had finally scampered off with the hideous caricature to show to my mother.

"Yes? What deed shall we do?"

"Let's pay our friend Martinez a visit."

"Pregnant idea, ol' cheroot! Simply pregnant."

"We can get two birds with one stone, ol' rhino snout. In the first place, we'll bring zest into the uneventful life of that lonely ol' grocer. In the second place, we'll make amends for having slighted the old boy on April Fool's Day. You know, he must have been as disappointed in us as the 40,000 were when we didn't come around and liven things up for him on that most significant occasion. Must be horrible, Sharkey, to be a lonely old bachelor like the Behemoth, passing a dismal existence in a mud hut."

"Yeah, horrible." And after a short reflection, Carl said, "As you have intimated, it's our Christian duty to mosey on over after dinner and arouse him from his miserable hibernation."

"Maybe we'd better have a meeting right now," suggested I, "and determine the will of the entire Royal Society concerning the matter."

" 'Nother pregnant idea, Left, down right fertile! You take over. I presided last time."

"The Royal Society of the Beebuzzards will now come to order," he announced. "The secretary will please read the minutes."

One leg dripping indolently over an arm of a squeaking rocker, Carl listened as a I pretended to read. "At the last meeting, March 2, the organization was called to order by the Right Reverend Carl Lewis, who called upon Right Honorary Secretary Lawrence Nelson to read the minutes. The said ex-con began as follows: `At the last meeting, held February 20, the organization was called to order by Reverend Padre Lawrence Nelson, who called upon his secretary, the untouchable Carl Lewis, to read the minutes.' "

"Let's return to the meeting in March, Lefty."

"Okay. `It was moved by one Lefty Nelson that, whereas, one Loyd McKinney had recently been declared mentally unbalanced and consequently dismissed from service at the First Methodist Church of Mesa, he should be reinstated by means of a petition to be sponsored by the Epworth League under the leadership of said Nelson and said Lewis. The motion was duly seconded by said Nelson and carried unanimously.' "

Later we were happy to find the mythical Beebuzzard Society 100 percent in favor of sending their co-presidents to call upon forlorn Mr. Martinez. And it was nice to know that our fellow members were always eager to back us in any movement we might design. How pleased we were when one, personified by Carl, likened our proposed deed unto "that of the Good Samaritan."

Another praised us for our part in having Mr. McPenny restored to his janitorship, and, all in all, we were highly complimented.

"Brothers," said I, assuming the role of another member, Snivel Jones, an acute adenoid case, "I reserve that ye air a lining up now to give yore co-presidents the right hand of corngracheelacheens. That air a right nice thing to do, but ye ain't thunk of one thing. If all us 40,000 souls give our brothers a personal corngracheelacheens, them two air a gonna be left with corns in their hands. Git it, brothers? That air air a pun!"

"I calculate then," continued he of the obstructed nasal passage, "that 'stead of planting corns and bunions in our brother's hands, we jist better up and give 'em three cornsarn cheers. Heh! Heh! I shore kin make them puns!"

After adjournment, we co-presidents went into conference. We decided that I would engage Martinez in conversation while Sharkey, equipped with a little hand generator we had extracted from my mother's obsolete telephone box, slinked to the man's chicken yard. There he...but why get ahead of the story?

After detailing our activities for the approaching afternoon, we were in the mood for recreation, and so I brought out the checker board with a proposition not unfamiliar to us both: "Winner gets the loser's dessert. Okay?"

"Okay."

This was a wager I was going to lose — and gladly, for losing my dessert was the first step in my scheme to secure revenge for the rice pudding incident at the Lewis domicile.

The game was in its last phase when Helen returned, and, sliding up to my guest, asked, "What you doing?"

"Putting your brother on a non-sugar diet, honey."

"Huh? What? What you doing?"

"Playing checkers, honey."

"What's checkers? Huh?"

"It's something you do when you want twice as much dessert as you ordinarily get."

"Huh?"

"Look, Helen," Carl beamed as he exchanged one of his blacks for two of my reds, "this is the way you play checkers."

"What you wanta do that for? Huh?"

"Oh, just to get your brother's goat."

"Bubber don't have a goat, don't you know? Huh? Why you wanta goat?"

"So I can have two helpings of dessert?"

"What's a dessert? You got a dessert?"

"Dessert is something like ice cream, or pie, or cake. Did your mother fix something like that for dinner?"

"She fixed pie."

"What kind of pie?"

"White pie."

"White pie?"

"Lemon with frosty meringue," I clarified.

"Yum, yum!" chortled the guest. "If there's anything I like better than a piece of lemon pie, it's two pieces of lemon pie."

"Mama say nice children don't be greedy like that," reproved Helen.

"Now, honey, you just run along now, and, when I finish beating Lawrence, I'll tell you the story of 'The Three Bears.' "

"I don't want you beat my brother! He might cry and get all dirty."

An emotional child, Helen brought Sharkey to this speedy compromise: "Okay, okay. I won't beat him; I'll be sweet to him and just vanquish him."

Vanquished soon afterward, I folded up the lacquered battlefield and with a pretense at vexation reminded, "There'll be another day, pal."

"Now then you tell me 'bout the free bears," ordered Helen as she climbed upon Carl's knee.

"Well," he began, "once there were three bears who lived in the woods. One day they sat down to eat some chile, and...."

"No, no, it was soup!" corrected Helen, quite obviously annoyed.

"Okay, it was soup."

Her annoyance gone, the child said with a giggle, "You don't know how to call the words."

"Well, when the three bears sat down to their soup, the big bear tasted his soup and said, 'This soup is too cold.' "

"No, it was too hot!"

It may have been that Carl couldn't recollect the infantile classics as they really should have been told and consequently made his sometimes extreme revisions in order to appear humorous and thereby cover up. Or it may have been that he made the changes in order to enjoy his listener's reactions.

Not until he reads this novel will he suspect that I sometimes wondered about his real knowledge of "Little Red Riding Hood," "Little Black Sambo," and a few others.

After reading the foregoing comments, it would be like Carl to do some research and establish his knowledge of bears by informing me that the characters in "the bear story were Euractos Americanus and, therefore, black bears rather than grizzlies, which are Ursus horribilis." The three personified bears were leaving their supper and about "to take a boat ride" when my mother called us to dinner.

Upon arriving at the dinner table, we heard my father's being scolded by my mother as he washed in the bathroom.

"Edgar," she said, "it's gotten to be a habit with you. Every day I have to call you a half dozen times before you'll leave off pitching that old fertilizer in the barn and come to dinner. You know very well Dr. Hogue advised you to rest an hour before and after noon each day."

"But, Lillian, can't you understand that it's just about an hour before lunch each day when the manure piles up so much? You don't realize how soggy the floor gets and how thick the flies are when I neglect the droppings."

"Oh, I'm so sorry you heard," said my female parent when she saw that the conversation was reaching our visitor.

"Oh, that's all right," replied the latter, and to me he murmured, "That farmy talk was just an appetizer, lad. So don't get encouraged and begin to think I'll leave your dessert for *you*."

During most of our meal we talked about Mr. Lewis' dairy and my father's cotton and corn he hoped to harvest in autumn. But eventually when all save a few survivors in a colony of frijoles had descended for expansion and the pork had moved on to human packing houses, our subject for discussion became the lemon pastry, which my mother declared to be the best she had cooked in years.

"Sharkey will have a double opportunity to test your work, mama," said I. "You see, he'll have my piece too."

"You're not going to try my pie, Lawrence, after I've labored and worked so long over that contrary old stove!"

Having sprinkled some grains of salt on the white meringue of Sharkey's and my dessert as I reached for meat and bread, I was willing to endure the inevitable chiding for "gambling" which followed my explanation about Sharkey's forthcoming double portion. I had revealed our checkers "agreement" so he'd be free and sort of obligated to eat in abundance.

Helen was the first to try the yellow-and-white product of my mother's culinary art.

"Um! Good pie!" were her exclamations. They were promptly echoed by the male head of the family.

Appearing to be looking elsewhere, I watched Sharkey as he dug eagerly into one of the slices before him.

"Boy, boy!" he exclaimed as he pulled an overloaded fork to his dental region. His jaws snapped shut, jogged one another like two pigs at the same trough, and then went into slow motion. Afterwards his face fell into an expression of misery.

"Don't you like mama's pie?" queried my little sister, plainly showing how horrible she would consider the guest were he to show other than keen liking for this delicacy.

"Why...sure...sure, it's swell, honey."

"Then why you don't eat some more?"

"I'm eating some more. I'm just taking my time so I can enjoy it longer."

"You lucky guy," I remarked, watching his countenance strain itself to stay untwisted. "Some guys get all the breaks!"

"Lawrence, I ought to let you do without," said my relenting mother, "but I'm not. I have just one more piece in the ice box you may have."

"Oh, keep that for Helen's supper and let Lawrence have my other piece, Mrs. Nelson" was Carl's hasty plea.

"No," I protested. "I'll not accept something I've already handed over as a forfeit. Either I eat the piece in the ice box or none at all."

Anxious argument from the checkers victor, my stubborn stand, mama's visit to the kitchen, and my subsequent delight.

When I finished my share of the delicious pastry, he of the sluggish jaws had consumed but little.

Just to see him drop his guard, I called the group's attention to a bird visible from the window at my father's back. "Strangest thing I've ever seen," I falsified to be sure they looked at the ordinary sparrow long enough to permit Sharkey a moment of facial relaxation.

Although my buddy robbed me of an unobstructed view of his contorted visage when he whipped out his handkerchief and emptied his mouth of its salty contents, my delight in seeing his distorted eyebrows and blinking lids was almost enough to assure me of retribution for the pudding affair.

For full measure, however, I said to Helen, "Look, little sis, Carl's not eating his pie as if he likes it. Mama's going to feel bad, if he doesn't like her good pie."

And before he could devise a reply, Helen's lips protruded in a fleeting pout, and then she screamed, "You gonna make my mama cry! You like that pie now!"

The parents' efforts to stop the child's ensuing flow of tears were not so successful as Carl's.

To this day I have admired the brave way in which he chewed self-sacrificially into the second part of his checkers winnings.

"Look, honey!" he said courageously, "I do like it! Yum, yum! Your mother is a fine cook!"

Who said that the day of martyrdom belongs to the distant past? Cramming his cheeks with a food that doubtless would have sent anyone but a hardened Beebuzzard outside to vomit, who was Sharkey but a martyr?

His ordeal finished, our hero pushed back his chair and tried to return Helen's smile. The little girl was happy now, for Carl had plainly showed his enthusiasm for her parent's cooking, and mama was not going to cry after all.

Half an hour after dinner, the wind grew weary of courting the sand with its wolfish whistling among the eaves and became so quiet that I could easily detect the rumbling in the reclining guest's upset stomach.

Tactfully explaining that, like my father and sister, he always took a little nap after lunch, the stricken one had stretched out on the sofa. He remained there until a series of cramps brought him up for a visit to the bathroom and a request for "a teaspoon of soda in a glass of water."

"Are you boys going to the show?" inquired my mother when she saw us putting on our sweaters.

"Sure are," said Carl. "And it's really going to be a dilly."

"What's on?"

"Oh, it's...it's something like 'Jostling the Behemoth,' I think."

"And it stars a couple of superb actors, mama, even though some people do say they're a pair of hams."

CHAPTER FOURTEEN

Chickens on the Wings

We were in the coupe and vibrating along to the beefy bachelor's grocery store when suddenly Carl applied the brakes, stepped out, and deserted the road.

"It's just as though I had taken a pint of castor oil," he complained from a clump of tumbleweeds.

"Must have been that soda," I suggested.

"Lefty, do you suppose...about that pie, lad, do you...."

"Carl, surely you're not actually going to say that my mother's cooking is to blame for your condition!"

"No, Left, I'm not blaming your mother's cooking, you understand, but I just wonder...weren't those lemons rather sour? Maybe I got too much acid. After all, I did eat two slices, you know."

"Say, boy," I asked of him 20 grunts later, "are you going to homestead it out there? Maybe I'd better fetch your trunk and tell your folks you've staked a claim and won't be home for awhile. Get the lead out, guy, and let's go!"

"Now, listen, lad, if you're getting impatient because you're getting chilly, just remember I'm not being furnished with a heater out here."

"No, but from all indications, I'd say you're working up a neat little sweat."

At last he came languidly back and crawled through the two strands of barbed wire, muttered a by-word because the little projections flirted sadistically with his backbone, and then joined me in The Carcass.

At the corner of Cedar and Main we were detained by a procession of Indians and a sprinkling of Hispanics.

Near the curb, burping Bernard Snerd was on hand to fumigate us with whiskey breath and to say, "Don't let those guys scare you, pals. They not gonna hurt anybody...no sire-ree!" Know what they're doin'? You guys are susch swell pals o'mine, I'm gonna let you in on a secret. Know what? Those guys are out guardin' cause this is Good Friday. They got an altar up on the mesa and they got lotsa men keepin' the devil away from it."

Armed with weapons ranging from pocketknives to baseball bats, the solemn group moved along in and out of step with a borrowed drum which inappropriately sported the name of a local dance orchestra.

"Let'em have it, fellas!" Snerd whooped after the "guards." "Scare the devil out of 'em!" And to a small unit of curious spectators, he said, "Man alive, but wouldn't you hate to be ol' Nick and see that gang comin' after you! They'd scare hell outa anybody!"

"Bet you guys wouldn't even known it was Good Friday," he said to us as we were on the point of rolling away, "if we hadn't gotten outa classes. Bet you're not even going to church. And I always thought you guys was susch swell pals and peachy Christians. How'n heck are you celebratin' Good Friday, anyway?"

"By visiting the lonely in heart, Snerd" was Carl's return as he pushed in on low gear. "And by staying sober, incidentally."

By the time we had reached our destination, my buddy had become so interested in the details we had been working out for Martinez that he forgot his nausea.

We parted at the side of the grocery before the owner had an opportunity to observe that one of us, Carl, had hurried to his back yard. Therein on the ground my fellow Beebuzzard would place a kernel of corn to whose two ends were attached a pair of very fine copper wires that made connection with our little telephone generator.

Our project would not be an experiment, for we had once tried it among my father's fowls and with feather-flying results.

Without waiting for the grocer to recognize me, I met him with the friendly reminder: "Mr. Martinez, I'm Alexander Hamilton, as you may recall. The honorable Thomas Jefferson and I bought some melons from you several months ago on behalf of The Royal Society of the Beebuzzards. Remember?"

"How you theenk I could ever forgate eet, Meester Alexhandgo?"

Perhaps when he reached for his knife he merely wanted to clean his nails.

Nevertheless, I lost no time in saying, "You don't know how sorry we were about all that, Mr. Martinez. We've been thinking lately how much we'd like to come back and change the bad opinion you, no doubt, have of us. Won't you please give us another chance to prove we're really a couple of nice fellows, Mr. Martinez?"

"The won time, Mr. Alexhandgo — I theenk eet was enough. Eef the mother of you had feefty pesos een the hand and you were weeth her when the lights say 'bye-bye' I theenk she wake up dead weeth the throat cut."

"Mister Martinez, do you know what I mean by conversion...getting religion, in other words?"

"Si, si. You mean when a fellow gate to be gude weeth God...do beesness weeth Heem weethout geeving to Heem the cheat."

"Well, then would you believe me if I were to tell you that Mr. Jefferson and I have gotten religion since we saw you last?"

"Eet might be possible," came the delayed reply. "Boat, how I gonna...."

"It happened just last week, Brother Martinez, and since that time we've been wanting to come over and give you the hand of fellowship and invite you over to our church, where our preacher, the Reverend Jasper O. Rice, is holding an Easter revival."

At this point I gripped his fingers in mine and squeezed until I heard a couple of joints pop.

"Won't you come over and just give Brother Rice a chance to work on you, Brother Martinez?" I continued. "He and his song leader, Brother McSkinny, would welcome you with open hearts. How about it, Brother Martinez? If you don't have a way, Brother Jefferson and I'll see that you get one."

He might be interested in coming, he said, but he wouldn't know until later. Saturday would be a busy day for him and he ought not to "loose so musch sleep."

"Well, at least, maybe you can come to the chicken barbecue Reverend Rice is having for everybody next Monday at 7:30 p.m."

"Monday?" He put his knife on a box of cheese and pinched his glossy cranium. "Maybe I can do thees. Quién sabe?"

"By the way, I told Reverend Rice that while I was visiting you I'd ask if you have some chickens to sell him for the barbecue. He said he's willing to pay big prices."

"Si, si, I got some cheekens. All kinds. Gude cheekens."

"Well, may I see them? He wanted me to look them over and tell him what I think of them."

"Si, si."

A steeple of canned peas jazzed timidly on the shifty floor as the ponderous man ushered me through an alley of goods to his poultry pen.

"I see you have both leghorns and Rhode Island Reds," I commented.

"Si, I got the Low Down Reds. I got all kinds of birds — white, red, browns. Boat I theenk you like the Low Down Reds best."

While Martinez' back was turned on his flock, Carl, hiding behind a shed, tossed a few oats near the kernel of wired corn and began turning the little generator.

The grocer was again facing his fowls when one of them rose from the ground, wildly beat her wings together, and cackled in shocked anguish.

"What's the matter with that `Low Down Red,' Brother Martinez?"

"I don' know." A worm of puzzlement wiggled in his brow.

It wiggled again when a second hen attained an elevation of four feet and cawed ravenlike above the mischievous grain.

"Eet mus be a boolsnake geeving my cheeks the scare," concluded Martinez as he waddled toward a crop of displaced feathers.

Carl pulled in the kernel so that it was gone when the fat one approached to search for a snake.

Forgive me, Carl, if I say that he should have looked for one behind the shed.

As the grocer rejoined me, our third victim, a leghorn this time, found the corn in another spot and, like her sister, reacted with the usual wing beating, squawking, and comb swinging.

"Brother Martinez, I'm not sure, but I'm afraid your birds have Chickarooka."

"Cheekarooka? Wot ees cheekarooka?"

"Why, Brother Martinez, I thought everyone knew about Chickarooka!"

"Wot thees theeng she do to my cheeks?"

"Well, finally they just get to be nothing but flesh and bone, and at last...well, they die."

"Boat, my fran, the cheeks they are all so fat and gude-luking."

"They are always fat in the first stages of the disease."

"I theenk the cheeks okay, Brother Alexhandgo. Tell you wot. Seence you want thees cheeks for the church, I'm gonna geeve you all you want for 35 cents."

"On behalf of the Reverend Jasper Rice, I want to thank you, Brother Martinez, and give you the right hand of fellowship."

He beat me to the squeeze this time and crowded my knuckles in a vice from which they were quite happy to gain liberation.

"Yes, my friend," I continued when the bone bending had ended, "you have shown the true Christian spirit by being so generous."

"Then we catch the cheeks, many cheeks, all of them, and take them queekly to thees meenester. No?"

"No, You see, Brother Martinez, I'm still afraid they have Chickarooka. And if they do, the people who eat them will take chicken pox. Now you certainly wouldn't want that, would you?"

"No, no. Boat theenk of all thees gude cheeks all gone to waste! And theenk of all the money I don' gate!" Ave Maria! Soon the cheeks all go to skeletons and then...then, by George, maybe I geeve up and go the pore houses queek."

Chin reaching for his chest, the sad man was leading the way back inside when he stopped, slapped at a fly, and appealed, "Boat couldn't you geeve the cheeks a long bake and keel thees germs?"

"Why, Brother Martinez, I'm surprise at you! Would you want to see all the good brethern die just to save you from going to the poor house?"

"No, no, but theenk...."

"Good morning, dear Brother Behemoth!" It was Carl.

Evidently Martinez still did not know that the uncommon word in the newcomer's salutation is used in Job to refer to an animal that was probably the hippopotamus, for he responded without malice, "Gude morning, Meester...I mean Brother Jeff."

"Brother Alexander," said Carl, "Brother Rice told me where you were and sent me with some money to buy forty-three hens. He said you could pay as high as two dollars each."

"Bad news," said I above the Latin's groan. "You see...say, Brother Martinez, Brother Jefferson can probably tell you all about Chickarooka. You see, he's studying to be a chianerian."

"A wot?"

"A chianrian. In other words, a fowl doctor."

Another running of frightened poultry, a seizure, an examination, and "Doctor" Lewis' grim diagnosis: "Chickarooka."

"Boat they are so gude-luking and fat!"

"Have faith, Brother Martinez," I urged. "There may be a cure."

"There is, indeed, a remedy for this perplexing situation, my prodigious friend. If you will adhere rigidly to precepts I shall prescribe you, you will observe a marked amelioration in the condition of the affected fowls and eventually you will note their complete recuperation."

"Wot you say, Meester Jeff?"

"I said if you'll do what I tell you to do, your chickens will be okay."

"Geeve eet to me, Brother Jeff, and you see I do eet!"

"Well, now what I'm going to tell you to do may seem crazy, but it has a real purpose. First, you must paint each bird's bill green."

"Catch each hen and paint hees beel green! Why I got to do thees, Meester Jeff?"

"Well, for one thing, that color has a good effect on the eyes. In the first place, however, we want to make the chicken thin. Now if her bill is painted green, she'll work off her fat trying to peck her own bill, which she thinks is a blade of grass. Moreover, the continual undulation of her neck will help circulate the red corpuscles from the cerebrum to the cerebellum and then to the medulla oblongata. The...are you listening, Brother Behemoth? You understand me, of course."

Why be estúpido all the time? This the man must have asked himself, for he answered, "Sí, sí!"

"Next you must soak each hen's feet for two hours in a mixture of peanut butter and molasses."

"Too bad, sad case, too bad!" I mourned in cadence with our funereal return to the interior.

"Boat, boat, can't I do soamtheeng else to make the cheeks go gude again? I do not have all thees time!"

"Why, yes, Mart," Carl said sharply, momentarily forsaking his brotherly approach, "just wring their confounded necks and bury 'em behind that stinking shed of yours."

"Forgive Brother Jefferson's unkind words, Brother Martinez," I besought as I nudged my buddy. "You see it was just last week he became a Christian and sometimes he forgets."

"I'm sorry, Brother Behemoth," apologized Carl.

"Eet ees notheeng. I forgeeve and forget."

"You fellows, you have some smokes?" He had held out a package of cigarettes.

"No thanks. We don't use them," declined Sharkey. "But we do like piñons."

"You help yourself."

Eagerly we delved into the keg of small pine nuts, filled our pockets, and then began cracking some between our teeth.

Piñons, usually gathered by Indians, are secured in two manners: They are either shaken from the trees that bear them or they are taken from squirrel nests. We observed with regret that the ones we were eating had been gotten from the latter.

Languishing on a low counter, the troubled one massaged a newborn headache, fanned neighborly flies, and began a monologue of self-pity.

"Two pesos each one," his favorite moan, expired in its fifth cycle when Carl, who had bitten into a little ball of animal waste he had thought to be a piñon, complained explosively. "For gosh sakes, Mart, why the devil don't you get the rat signs out of these nuts!"

"Those not rat peels! They only squirrel! You don't pay for them. I gave them to you. So why you fuss?"

"Please, brothers!" I pacified. "Remember we are all brothers despite race, creed, or color. Let us remember the Golden Rule:

'Whatsoever you would that men should do to you, do ye even so to them.' Now then, brothers, let's say that together."

Immediately after the three of us repeated the scripture, I said, "Now then, Brother Jefferson, don't you think you should say that you're sorry for your hasty words? And, Brother Martinez, don't you feel sorry about yours?"

I always admired the way in which Carl cracked knuckles. In the handclasp which came now after a caboose of muttered apologies from the two transgressors, the poppings were like notes from an untuned xylophone, but to the ears of a Beebuzzard they were somewhat musical.

"You're losing weight, Brother Behemoth," remarked Sharkey, mercifully releasing the bulky one so that his circulatory system might resume its work.

"You theenk so?"

"No doubt about it. Have you been sick lately?"

"No."

"Well, you look as if you'd been in bed with some kind of serious illness. Don't you think he looks bad, Brother Nel...I mean Brother Alexander?"

"Well, yes, he does. I noticed it when I first saw him this afternoon, but I didn't want to make him feel bad by saying anything about it. I thought maybe he'd just gotten over typhoid fever."

"Boat, boat, fellows, I been feeling gude...at least, until I find out my cheekens all got thees Cheekarooka."

The big specimen of perfect health lumbered to a mirror on the refrigerator and looked at himself.

"Don't you see how pale you are?" asked Carl.

"He certainly is pale," I put in. "But it's really those dark circles under his eyes that worry me, Brother Jefferson."

Suddenly my buddy was alarmed. "Quick, tell me, Brother Martinez, have you, by any chance, eaten any of your chickens during the past week or so!"

"Sí, I eat a leetle Low Down Red last Soanday."

"Let's see now...one, two, three, four, five days! That's exactly the time in which one exposed to rasslemuletoe baciliorukas shows indications of having contracted said rasslemuletoe baciliorukas."

I was amused to see that Carl, who had just on the spur of the moment coined this ungodly medical name for our non-existing disease, had been able to repeat it without error and without faltering.

"Wot you say, Meester Jeff?"

88

"In other words, Brother Behemoth, I am very sorry to tell you that you have Chickarooka."

"Me! Cheekarooka! No, my fran, you...you really theenk I got her?"

A solemn nod from "Brother Jeff." Another examination in the mirror. And this time the man's face really *was* pale.

"It's plain as the knob on his face that he's in bad shape," I said low enough to give the impression he was not to have heard the cheerless comment.

A hopeless shake of Carl's head and then his belief: "The man ought to be in a hospital."

Seated again, Martinez said, "Boat don't I got cheeken poz? I thought you said a...."

"Well, yes," I interrupted. "It is true, as I said before, that a person who eats a fowl infected with Chickarooka will have chicken pox, but the chicken pox gotten from a chicken rather than another person is so serious and so much worse than ordinary chicken pox that we just call it plain old Chickarooka."

"Well, now I wouldn't say the disease can't be cured, Brother Hamilton," said my colleague. "I once knew a man who had it and got well again. Peculiar thing how all of his four children got it while his wife escaped it."

"And hees four keeds? They got well? No?"

"No, they...uh...died."

He was reaching for the telephone when Carl stopped him.

"Wait, dear Brother Martinez," he implored. "You haven't the money to be calling doctors. After all, your hens will be dead in a few weeks, you'll be in bed and unable to make money, and you'll have to hire a girl to come here and wait on you. You don't have any money to be shelling out to some doctor. He'd charge you a huge fee for a case like this. And, moreover, he'd send you to the hospital. And you know how it is there. The nurses won't pay you any attention. They spend all their time attending to young, handsome men. They'd just let an old ugly critter like you waste away and dry up while they pampered some good-looking football player with a sprained ankle."

"You mean they...they let me...uh...die?"

"Of course, they would! And they'd send your relatives a big bill they wouldn't be able to pay. And if they didn't pay the bill, one of them would have to go to jail."

"Brother Martinez, did you ever live on nothing but bread and water?" It was my turn to work on the bachelor. "Do you want that for one of your relatives? Surely you're not going to send one of your good relatives to prison to be starved and tormented! What would Reverend

Rice think of a man so selfish, so unkind, so cruel? Why he wouldn't even preach your funeral.

"And nobody else would even go to your funeral. Since you'd be proverty stricken, the city would just have somebody haul your body in a truck out to the cemetery. After paying all they could on your hospital and doctor bills, your poor relatives wouldn't have money enough to buy you a casket. They'd just have to roll you up in a blanket, dump you in a hole, and cover you up. In fact, you might not even have a place in the cemetery. It costs money, you know, to buy even a little plot there. They might have to bury you out on the mesa. Now how'd you like to have some badger digging down and stacking your bones as if they were poker chips, or how'd you like to have some burro pawing and braying over your unmarked grave topped by bitterweeds and grasshoppers?"

Surely no man, I thought to myself, was ignorant and dull-witted enough to swallow all this, but apparently the Behemoth was, for he said in all seriousness, "Boat, gentlemen, I got insurance, and maybe...."

"Makes no difference how much insurance you have," discouraged Carl. "It would all go for something else. Why, the local health unit would say you sold chickens with Chickarooka and thereby gave the disease to others, and they'd sue your beneficiaries and your kinsmen down to your fifth cousin."

"Yes, and a mob would probably run them out of town. Brother Jefferson is right."

Broken and spiritless, the convention of human lard settled on an upturned keg, submitted his greasy head to the flies, and moaned pitiably, "I cannot afford to stay leeving and I cannot afford to die. And I cannot tell nobody I got thees Cheekarooka. What I'm gonna do?"

"Courage, dear Brother Behemoth! Brother Hamilton and I will ask Brother Rice to pray for you."

"And Brother Jefferson will treat you free of charge."

"I shall be very happy to treat you, Brother Behemoth."

"You fellows, you are so kind to me. Have all the piñons you want. If only you feex me up from dying, I geeve you a whole bushel of piñons...and I personally weel peek out all the squirrel peels."

"My friend, if you'll just carry out my instructions, I'll swear to you on the sacred manual of the Beebuzzards that within five days you won't know yourself."

His hope revived, the grocer renewed his feud with the flies, dared another glance in the mirror and then wheeled to ask, "Boat, Meester Jeff, I don' got to paint the nose green, do I?"

"Oh, no, of course not. But we've got to get that weight off—fast."

Just before we left him in his closed store an hour later, the three of us agreed to tell no one of our patient's illness. We would cure him and then he could treat his "cheeks" and no one would go to the "pore houses or the jail or gate the body poot in a hole on the mesa," and we would be "gude fellows and eat lots of piñons!"

Sometimes at night just before I fall into slumber I see him again doing a stationary run in a bathtub of molasses and peanut butter, and, as torrents of perspiration half blind the puffing man, I hear him heaving like a walrus afflicted with bronchitis, and I hear an order from Sharkey: "Get the lead out, Brother Mart!"

And then as the sandman covers my lids with a few more grains from his sleep potion, I see the Behemoth pounding his bulges with a rolling pin and I hear the voice of his "doctor" call out, "Harder, Mart! Beat it off! You wanta live, don't you? Don't just stand there like a jackass on a iceberg!"

Then comes Mart's laborious reply. "Eet ees easy to seant and eet the piñons, boat you try beeting the belly weeth the club and jumping up and down een theese mess and, by George, you forget you are a Creestian!"

And finally I hear myself appealing, "Peace brothers! Say you're sorry for your harsh words." The apologies, the knuckle cracking, the slosh of syrup, the thud of hickory on fat, and then the genie of folklore blows out my light of consciousness, leaving the sign MARTINEZ GROCERY swinging in the wind of memories.

CHAPTER FIFTEEN

Behold, We Are Two Wayfarers

Not so many mornings after we had secured the Behemoth's pledge of eternal gratitude for "feexing me from dying," Carl and I played hookey from Sunday School to make a trip to Old Rusty, the snaggle-toothed peak in the distance that for sometime had seemed challenging us to scale its rocky knob and sit beneath its quintet of pines that appeared not unlike a great eye winking at all who would look up from Mesa and behold Nature flirting for companionship.

Our destination was but 15 miles away and we would be gone for a mere six hours, but Sharkey's father insisted that we go well provisioned.

"Now let's see," he said, looking in the rump of The Carcass, "you boys got the two gallons of water I pumped for you, and you have the gallon of motor oil, two spare tires, plenty of cup grease, and a coupla extra gallons of gas. Now let me think. Is there anything else you oughta have along?"

"That's enough, dad, for gosh sakes! We're not going to China or Africa, you know — just Bobcat Canyon, a mere frog leap from here."

"See how he is, Lawrence?" said the parent. "He's too much like I am — too chance-takin.'"

"Yeah," said Carl, "dad's a regular daredevil."

"And it's too bad," Mr. Lewis regretted. "But I always was one of these fellas that'll take a chance and try *anything* once. By the way, you boys better wear some colored glasses in this glare, and it might be a good idea to carry some kinda lotion to keep from blistering in this heat. Better mind what I say now."

"We're used to the sun, dad. Yes sir, Lefty, my dad is a daredevil of the first magnitude...reckless as a bull reaching puberty."

Mrs. Lewis came out to caution us about being wary of rattlesnakes and to reprove us again for not first attending church "and then going on your outing."

"It's okay, mother. We'll be out admiring God's handiwork, His great outdoors."

"But its Communion Sunday, you know."

"Well, I hope Lefty's Cousin Boyd behaves himself today," said the son in what was probably an attempt to tease me. "Mother, the last time we had communion, the man came in loaded with his cough medicine, crashed a fortification of ushers, and as he stumbled down the aisle toward the little containers of grape juice, he said, 'The drinks are on the house, men! Set'em up, Brother Goodman, 'cause we're comin' and gittin' 'em!'"

Good ol' Carl, I thought sarcastically. How proud he made me feel in the presence of others of my imbibing relative. Well, I consoled myself, there was more salt in my mother's kitchen.

"Don't worry about our not going to church, Mrs. Lewis," said I. "We'll stop by and get a dose of religion from old Uncle Thomas."

"You mean that queer old darkey who lives in the foothills...the one who sees visions?"

"The very same." As I answered I glanced behind the seat and saw that we had not forgotten a pair of sheets which we would need for our call on the black one. They rested quietly along side our .22's and two bags of luncheon.

"Long live the Beebuzzards!" we reiterated as the Model T tapped into the gravel road and nosed toward the purple mountain in the east.

And finally we invited the 40,000 to join us in our official battle hymn, which we sang nasally to the tune of "Anchors Aweigh." A source of inspiration to every member of the Society, it was:

> "Wha, wha, wha, wha, wha-wha,
> Wha, wha, wha-wha!
> Wha wha, wha, wha, wha, wha
> Wha hoodle a who, a hoodle a who, a wha!"

Jolting along the mesa, we opened our nostrils to the faint but definite fragrance of newly-leaved mesquite bushes and the mild piquancy of greasewood.

Coyotes that looked up red-toothed and shame-faced, after feasts of lamb, and vanished through concealing arroyos whiles steers rambling among spiny cacti lowed their relief...wakeful prairie dogs that unselfishly shared subterranean apartments with owls and snakes and watched at the entrance of their abodes while sluggish jack rabbits observed premature siestas.

Visible here were hawks that preyed upon timid ground squirrels while nervous lizards tiptoed across warm dunes to leave grotesque patterns which tripped dungy tumble bugs.

Here we could hear crows that tried to bully the heavens with their brazen raucousness while cooing doves called for armistice and tiny wild canaries piped delicate approval.

This was our mesa, paradise for the Beebuzzards, home of the 40,000.

Gone here were our thoughts of approaching final examinations, of dictatorial Bossy Betsy, of the haughty toe-heads.

For this was our land of freedom...our hunting grounds, our place of wiener roasting and marshmallow toasting, a place where we could raise our voices unheard above a summer melon or lie relaxed at night upon a quilt and try to decode a coyote's message to the moon.

Here we could sit quietly beside an autumnal yucca dancing in a dress of consuming flame and hear dry mesquite beans teletyping in the breeze the message that this expanse of undefiled desolation did not play second fiddle in the consideration of the Creator, for He created it before He created man.

I was thinking of Alice and remembering that she would soon be returning to Mesa when The Carcass came to a slow-down before a cattle guard, where a scowling man cast away the butt of a homemade cigarette and demanded, "One dollar, if you want to pass through my property."

"But we won't hurt your land," reasoned Carl. "We don't want to lease it, pard. We just want to pass through it to the springs, where we're going to visit old Uncle Thomas and maybe climb to the pines."

"You guys know that ol' black man?"

"No, but we've been told about him, and we'd rather like to see him," replied Carl.

"One dollar, right here then. Or in plain language — one buck." The swarthy rancher raised his rugged high cheek bones in an expression of insolent stubbornness and placed his sinewy hands on his hips.

"Okay, you win," said I as I tossed him a quarter.

"Hey, wait a minute, you! I said a dollar, and you gimme 25 cents."

The Ford was whining in low when its driver assured him, "That's a dollar, fella. You're just far-sighted."

He was in a cloud of dust and looking in his palm when I last saw him.

"I have a feeling," said Sharkey, "that lad is going to give us trouble."

"He did seem like a nasty type."

At the springs we parked in an alcove of willows and made preparations for our climb.

We were about to take our guns and lunches with us when we altered our plans and decided to leave them and take only the white linens. First, we would visit the visionary hermit and then we would return to the car for equipment needed in the mountain scaling.

Endless cactus plants, tumbleweeds, scrubby pines, and degenerate mountain oaks allied with variegated boulders and ghostly slabs of towering rock to camouflage the little path we had been told would lead us to the abode of long withdrawn-from-it-all Thomas.

At last we descended into a little valley among the foothills and caught sight of a crude adobe hut thatched by an upheaval of willow limbs and cedar twigs that loomed in the distance like the ruffled head of a scarecrow.

"No wonder that old Negro sees visions," remarked Carl. "Look at that place, Left. If I had to live there all by myself, I'd be lonely as a skunk in a floral shop." Then after a pause, he said, "Well, we'd better take off shirts and pants and put on our Arabian attire, don't you think?"

"Right. And just before we get there, we'd better kick off our twentieth-century shoes, too."

Moments later we came barefooted, wrapped in sheets, and hallooing to the doorway of the seclusive one, who, like an inquisitive chipmunk out of his hole, came hobbling in his faded overalls to meet us.

"Behold, we are two wayfarers," said Carl, "journeying from afar."

"Yes, even so," agreed I. "we are two shepherds from Jerusalem who have worn out good camels and good asses to reach thee."

"Verily we have brought thee a message from Saint Bernard and Saint Vitus Dance."

He was still standing there and squinting at us when I said, "We beseech thee to open thy house unto us, for we are weary and the hot pebbles push unpleasantly upon mine corns."

"Yes, get thine lead out!"

The Negro's pupils continued to widen in their embankments of white and swim in a mute sea of wrinkles.

At last he broke his silence by cracking a rheumatic knee on the ground and raising his voice and eyes to the heavens with: "Laud, you done answered mah prayer! Yas suh, Ah thank thee Laud, 'cause you done sent me dese messengers."

"If Saint Bernard and Saint Vitus Dance were here," spoke Shepherd Lewis, "they would advise thee at this point, Thomas, to rise and go in peace."

"Dat's 'zactly what Ah gonna do, Mista Shepherd. An' Ah gonna ask yo and yo friend to come in an' rest yoself and gimme dat message."

Pointing to a bench in the meagerly furnished room, he was about to lower himself on an apple box when I caught his arm and said, "Know ye not, Thomas, that 'tis sinful to sit with the hams raised above the heel?"

"Yea, verily," Carl reinforced, "Saint Bernard and Saint Vitus Dance would not sit in such a fashion."

"Then how'm Ah gonna sit, Mista Shepherd?"

"Sit in this manner," I replied, sinking to the dirt floor and crossing my legs before me.

Had I not been watching, I might have thought that the groaning visionary was wrestling with a chiropractor, for his slow squat to the hard ground sounded like a popcorn heater in slow motion.

At length the demons of rheumatism stopped playing hockey in the toothless one's joints and let him whine down to a comfortable gum sucking.

"How 'bout dat message from dem saints?" he whistled when he had regained sufficient breath to enable him to speak.

"Be of patience and good cheer, my son," admonished Shepherd Lewis, "for ye shall have it in due time."

"How come you call me 'mah son,' Mista Shepherd? I 'spect Ah is 'bout 45 year older dan yo is."

"Nay, my son, time hangs heavily upon my brow and that of Shepherd Nelson here. We are pilgrims from many centuries of the past, wayfarers from the land of Sloppymoppy, where the men are not burdened by beards and the women are bald."

"But...but, Ah thought you all was from Jerusalem."

"Sloppymoppy is a suburb of Jerusalem, where we met Saint Bernard and Saint Vitus Dance. And they did tell us to come unto thee here in thy mountainous retreat and say unto thee what Shepherd Lewis shall say unto thee. But first, have ye no drink to offer us?"

"Yea, my son, our tongues are truly parched and needs must be moistened or be unyielding as brittle sticks before the hearth."

In a window of the two-room shanty hung three jugs which were each covered with cotton fabric and saturated with water.

"Ah keep dese wet so dey ain' gonna be so hot," explained Thomas as he tilted the middle container and allowed a pink beverage to trickles into a tin cup, which, when it was full, he handed to my companion.

"My son," said the latter, after he had sampled the drink, "fall upon thine knees and ask thy Savior for forgiveness for offering strong wine unto famished wayfarers."

"Dat ain' wine...yet, Mista Shepherd. Dat is jest some juice of some wild grapes an' it's jest a lil' bit tart, but dat's all."

"Then ye were keeping it until it did become strong wine, is it not so? Lie not to me, my son, for I have the wisdom of a prophet."

"Yas suh, but Ah prays yo fo'giveness, and Ah likewise prays de Laud's fo'giveness." Again he cracked down on one knee and looked upward. When he had finished his supplication, he emptied the tin cup of its contents and filled it with water from another jug.

"I shall not drink until that vessel containing the substance that will become strong wine be poured upon the ground."

When Thomas appeared hesitant, Carl, added forcefully, "then if ye are not willing to heed my wish, we shall depart this moment and go straightway unto the saints."

As if he had suddenly received an intravenous injection from the fountain of youth, the aged one jerked down the jug of juice and sent it shattering on an outside boulder. "Please, Mista Shepherd Men," he begged, "please don' tell dem saints. Heahafter, I ain' never gonna have nothin' in dis house but water. Ah swears Ah ain'."

"Fear not, my son, for thou art forgiven. Now give drink unto Shepherd Nelson, for he is sorely hot, and his teeth do burn like unextinguished butts upon an ash tray."

'Twas not meet, thought I, that our host be relieved so quickly, and so I said, "Thomas, I canst not accept water from one who cuts the brush from his face. Know ye not that 'tis sinful to shave the brush from thy face?"

"Yea, verily," supported Sharkey, "Saint Bernard and Saint Vitus Dance did not so."

"Ah dint' know dat. Ah swear Ah dint' know dat!"

It should be quite understandable why his orchestra of cracking joints and grunts were in greater harmony this time as he dipped low again and again countenanced a picture of penitence to the sky, for this was the man's third or fourth concert in the dirt. Or, as a sports announcer might say, it was the fourth down coming up.

Now that we had quenched our thirst, Carl expressed our hunger and asked, "Have ye naught to sop, oh thou dweller in a land of rocks and thorns?"

"Yas suh...Ah means, yea, verily."

Was the old one going to try his tongue at Biblical speech?

Evidently he was, for he added, "Ye gonna sho 'nough like mine barbecued terrapin."

"Have ye nought else?" said I with the hope that I had not shown my extreme distaste.

"Ye ain' gonna want nothin' else when you gits a sight of dat delicious terrapin Ah done cooked up and plastered wid chile sauce and garlic."

"How right ye are, my son." The garlic alone would have repelled Sharkey. Long ago I had had to choose between it and his friendship.

"Laud, but Ah sho had a time puttin' the flame to dat critter. Ever time Ah throwed 'im on dem burnin' sticks he up and crawl out. You...Ah mean, ye oughta seen dat tussle me an' him had. Firs' Ah would kick 'im in, and den he'd pull out dem ol' legs o' his an' march out like the debil was behind 'im wid his pitchfork. Finally when it look like Ah was gonna git blistas all over mah feet pushin' dat ol' turtle bak in dat fire, den Ah calls on de Laud fo' hep.

"And lo and behold de Laud say, 'Thomas, git yoself a pole, and eber time dat terrapin crawl out dem coals, you poke 'im back in wid dat pole.' And, good shepherds, Ah cut me a willow stick. And de Laud was wid me and Ah kept shovin' dat critter back til de fire frizzled his ol' legs and he give up de ghost and settle down like a real believer on dem coals just like he knowed he was gonna be et by messengers from dem saints. What you say dem saints is called? Saint Behard and Saint Biteus?"

Being humane toward all dumb animals, I lost no time in rebuking him for his cruelty. "Thomas, know ye not that ye must not kill in such a manner? Kill swiftly so that thy prey dies with but little suffering. Suppose ye were a terrapin and some creature having more power than thee rammed thee into a fire? Wouldst thou enjoy roasting in agony and smelling thine own belly sizzling on the flame?"

"But ye done fogit de Laud done tell me to git dat pole."

"Nay, my son," spoke up Carl. " 'Twas but the voice of Satan, who was disguising himself to make thee do this wicked thing and send thee into a fire much hotter than that of thy barbecue pit."

"You mean Ah ain' heard de Laud on dis matta?"

"Nay, nay," I assured the perturbed one. "The Lord does not utter words that cause anyone to torment his creatures."

"Yas suh, but it weren't nothin' but a lil' ol' terrapin...nothin' but a lil' ol' stinkin' critter de rain water wash down from dem peaks over yonder. De Laud ain' gonna denouce me fo' dat, is he? Say it ain' so, Mr. Shepherd men from — where yo say yo is?"

"From the distant land of Sloppymoppy, oh thou of the midnight snout," reminded Carl, and I tacked on: "Where the men do not sin by cutting their beards — because they have none — and the women are always bald."

"Ah ain' gonna sin no mo' by cutting' mah beard, Mista Shepherds. Honest I ain'. Look, heah what Ah gonna do."

Before we could stop him (as if we would) the old fellow hurled his razor and shaving mug against an outside boulder, and as pieces of the glass responded with a coquettish tinkle to the embrace of gravity, he cried out, "Now den, de Laud's gonna fo'give me fo' burnin' dat ol' turtle, ain' he? Ah ain' gonna shave no mo'...not even if mah beard gits so long I got to tie it around mah neck!"

"It were better, my son, that ye hanged thyself with it, for ye are a man of many trespasses. What think ye, Shepherd Nelson, of this matter?"

"I think we should straightway communicate with Saint Bernard and Saint Vitus Dance to learn whether or not there be some kind of self-chastisement Thomas may inflict upon himself in order to gain redemption of his soul."

"Yea, verily, the saints will tell us how he can be delivered out of the furnace of eternal brimstone. But first, let us eat. My son, have ye nought else to offer us? Give us a bountiful repast, for thy salvation depends upon our communication with the saints, and we cannot communicate very well with unsatisfied stomachs."

"Yas suh! Ah got two cans o' good ol' sardines and some sodee crackers, and fo' dessert Ah got some honey Ah catched from wild bees on up de canyon. Laud, but dem bees sho put de stinger to me when Ah got dat honey! Mista Shepherds, weren't no comfortable place Ah could sit down on fo' a week."

Abruptly he changed subjects and said in a worried voice, "Mista Shepherd, Ah'd do anything to get back on de side o' de Laud. Me and Him been runnin' dis lil' corner o' de earth ever since He come out from behind a rock one day all shining to beat six bits and say, 'Thomas, put down dat goat ye done stole from your neighbor an' fall down on yo back and repent before Ah sticks thee wid a bolt o' lightnin' and creates a black cinder out o' yo hide.' "

At last the tender sardines lay stretched out in a bowl on the crude table in company with a platter of faded crackers and a jar of dark honey.

Our host was about to go outside for another box to serve as an additional chair when Sharkey stopped him with: "Nay, my son. Know ye not that 'tis not meet to eat upright. Ye must lie down to sop in this manner."

Confound Carl! This ground was hard as a carbuncle on a head hunter's trophy, and it seemed to me that we had been wallowing on it long enough. Nevertheless, I responded, "Yea, verily, Saint Bernard and Saint Vitus Dance would surely condemn us if we did not salt ourselves with soil while we sop." But, perhaps after all, hearing and seeing the ebony one in another chiropractic adjustment would compensate for my own discomfort.

We bowed our heads while our host asked the blessing. "Laud," he said, "we thanks ye that ye done growed dese fish fo' our entrails to take hold of and put marrow and meat on our frames. An' we thanks ye fo' dis other stuff...stuff like de honey dem bees done squeezed out fo' us to consume.

"An', Laud, changing de subject jest a lil' bit, Ah ain' gonna put de torch to no mo' terrapins. Ah wouldn' done it dat time, but Ah thought dat was Yo dat come out dat bush. It was gittin' late, Laud, and Ah guess it was a lil' bit too dark fo' me to see dat was the debil 'stead of' Yo. Now, Laud, whatever Yo...Ah mean, Thou tellest me to do to git back in Yo good graces Ah gonna sho do, an' if Yo speaks through dem saints and dese shepherds git de message, Ah gonna do it, whatever it be, an' Ah ain' jest jostlin' Yo, Laud. Now lead us safely through dis meal and evermo.' Amen!"

"Thomas," said I, "think ye that thy blessing has reached the ears of thy Creator?"

"Course, Mista Shepherd Man, ain' nothin' He can't heah. Why de Laud can heah a worm crawlin' on a piece o' polished agate. Yas suh, an' He can heah de heartbeat o' a gnat!"

"'Tis not a question of His Power, Thomas," I replied. "'Tis simply that He has turned a deaf ear to thy speech. Thou must redeem thyself before He will listen to thee again."

"My son, just as soon as we have sopped," said Carl, "we shall communicate with Saint Bernard and Saint Vitus Dance that they must instruct us in the chastisement thou must inflict upon thyself in order to be forgiven of thy sins, namely that of torturing the defenseless terrapin. Now for the present, eat heartily, for soon thou will probably be in dire need of much strength."

I do not to this day know why Carl was encouraging our victim to "eat heartily." Could he not observe that there was not sufficient food for the three of us?

Thomas had taken aim and was leaning forward to fork a sardine when I took matters in hand and arrested his movements with: "Stop! Let there be silence! Me thinks I hear the voice...yea, it is the voice of Saint Vitus Dance! Let us bow our heads and listen."

Taking advantage of a rustling sound made in the roof, no doubt, by insects, I said, "Thomas, hear ye not the spiritual voice of Saint Vitus?"

"Ah don' heah nothin', Mista Shepherd," he acknowledged "'cept dat scratching sound."

"God help thee, Thomas, for thou has spoken irreverently of the sacred voice of Vitus Dance."

"Yea, verily, my son," agreed Sharkey, "thou hast cast more brimstone into the furnace thou shalt surely inhabit in hell."

"Pray fo' me, Mista Shepherd Men! Pray fo' dat ol' charcoal soul o' mine! Ah ain' meant no harm. Ah wouldn't said dat if Ah had knowed dat saint was talkin'. Ah thought dat was some worms crawlin' in dem willow poles."

"May the Lord have mercy on thy soul, Thomas!" I ejaculated. "Dost thou not realize thou hast just compared the holy Saint Vitus with a worm?"

"Oh, mercy, Laud! Laud have mercy 'pon mah po' soul!"

At this point our miserable host arose and threw himself headlong upon his cot of orange crates and gunny sacks and wailed until I said, "Thomas, 'tis not meet to rest upon ought save the ground?"

He desisted then and again begged me to ask Saint Vitus Dance what he must do to make amends for his transgressions.

Calling upon Shepherd Lewis to do likewise, I shut my eyes and went into meditation. What to have him do—that was the question. What about having him spank himself with a thorny mesquite limb? Or what about having him lie ten minutes in an ant hill? Or perhaps it might be better to have him rub his nose with a piece of sandpaper. But we didn't have any sandpaper, and, besides, the thing might be somewhat barbarous. The other two might also be barbarous...at least for today, for today was Sunday.

Inspiration came to me finally when I raised my head and beheld a ballet of heat waves radiating above a rusty barrel that lay basking in the May sun.

"Thomas," said, I, "Saint Vitus Dance says for thee to arise, strip thyself down to a loincloth, and bend thy body over yonder hot barrel that dost now drink in the sweet sunbeams in thy turnip garden. Thou must rest solely upon the metal and neither feet nor hands must touch the ground. In this position thou wilt feel, somewhat, that which the poor terrapin felt in thy barbecue pit."

Munching crackers and tasty sardines, we watched the groaning one seesawing on the big drum, while trying to balance himself to avoid receiving too much heat on his distressed middle.

Yes, it was Sunday, and when we two wayfarers from afar had finished our sopping I would further show how Christian I was by plastering Thomas' parched skin with a salve made of honey and sardine oil, "a balm used by the physicians in Sloppymoppy, where the men had no beards and the women were bald."

CHAPTER SIXTEEN

Suping in the South

The school term was over and the Beebuzzards, happy as a pair of
fledglings just out of downy confinement, were many miles east of
western Rusty and the valley over which he stood his jovial vigilance.

"Green as a gourd," remarked Sharkey as he looked over the fresh
expanse of my grandfather's southland farm that lay coddled in the
arms of twilight.

The Carcass sneezed in the fragrant dampness, jogged on a carpet
of clay ridges, and proceeded anew with its serenade of rattling up the
squirmy ruts in the pasture. Uncle Boyd had lost a wager, for he had
bet that the vehicle would not reach our destination, that it would
become an inmate in a junk asylum or would become an apartment
house for rodents and insects somewhere along the highway.

A cow, switching its buttocks in a perpetual game of tag with
annoying gnats, stalked leisurely out of the way and lowered her head
for another mouthful of bermuda.

We stopped finally before a pale blue frame house that stood on
cement haunches and peered at us from windows weak with age.

Physically they were an incongruous twosome — short and
chubby "Granddo" McCord, my maternal parent's father, in his late
seventies, and his tall and bony son, Filbert, in his early thirties.
Mentally, however, they were less incongruous.

Now the sole occupants of the musty old place that had once
sheltered the large McCord family, the two stood on the porch and
watched us come to a standstill just outside the front yard gate.

Finally Filbert grinned slowly out to meet us.

"You git heah in that thing?" he queried through a set of yellow
teeth.

Granddo, bringing up the rear, took my hand and dutifully began
to inquire about us all, and so I did not have a chance to answer his
offspring's question.

"Reckon you boys need some vittles," he suggested finally through
a faded mustache that looked as if it had gone to too many coffee

dunkings. "We were just gittin' ready to set down. That gull...what's her name?...I mean yer maw, said you'd git here this mawning. What kept you up? Charles, run on and finish fixin' them eggs."

"For shuck's sake, papa, quit callin' me Charles! That ain't my name. That's my brother's name. Shucks, that's all you do — try to make a dern fool outa somebody. Can't you call the words right?"

"Don't make no difference what I said. You know what I meant. Git them...git that stuff ready and les eat breakfast."

"You crazy ol' fool! It ain't breakfast...it's supper."

"Gad, it don't make no difference what I said. Gwan and git it ready, I say."

"Papa, I work too hard. Everybody says I need a vacation."

"Get out with that stuff, you crazy dunce you! Don't need no such a thing. By gad, all you do is fix eggs and wash dishes. Niggas do everything else." The pink wrinkles in the father's face arose to express his irritation.

While the eggs rattled in the kettle, Granddo rambled on. "We got a phone. Heard over the phone them Republicans...."

"You don't mean a phone," corrected Filbert, "you crazy ol' fool. You mean a radio. Why can't you call the right word? Shucks, I got ten times as much sense as you got."

"Shut up, you crazy dunce, and fix that stuff. That fella said the Republicans was gonna try and run the country."

"What fellow was that, Granddo?" I asked.

"Pshaw, that fella. You know!"

"Crazy ol' fool means that radio 'nouncer," clarified my uncle.

The eggs and corn bread and buttermilk ready, we bowed our heads with Granddo and Filbert.

"Lord, we thank ya for this stuff and everything," said Granddo, "and, Lord, we thank thee for the Republicans....I mean, we don't want them to run the country like we want to do if the...that is...what I mean...."

"Pshaw," he said finally in self disgust, "I forgot the whole danged thing."

To detract from his embarrassment, he railed at his son with: "These eggs are too hard, Charles...I mean, Filbert. Can't you tell time, you crazy dunce you?"

"You think I can't tell time, papa? You're crazy. Everybody knows I sure could spell when I was in the third grade."

"Yeah, but you never did go past the fourth grade, you crazy dunce.

"Papa, why'n heck don't you git 'at nasty buttermilk outa yo beard? That makes mah stomick git all sick inside."

"Don't make no difference 'bout that. Gwan, an' eat yer breakfast...supper, I mean."

"'Nother thing, you oughta quit spittin' on the floor, papa."

"Gwan and eat yer...yer stuff there."

"You have a pretty place here, Mr. McCord," said Carl, cutting in on the bandying between father and son.

"Ain't nothin' what it used to be, er...what's yer name again?"

"Lewis."

"Lees?"

"Papa can't understand nothin'. He can't 'member nothin' either, can you, papa?"

"Course I can, you crazy dunce. I can remember lotsa things — things like a lotta wild turkeys heahabouts and all kinsa other wild stuff that ain't heah now. Ain't nothin' on the place. Filbert's done run 'em all off poppin' off with that little air gun o' his."

"You crazy ol' fool, don't you know I ain't had no air gun since you got mad an' wrapped it 'round 'at hickory 'bout three or two years ago? Shucks, papa, what you wanta do that for? Huh? I wasn't doing nothing', 'cept shootin' flies on Niggas. Ain't nothin' wrong with that."

"Them Niggas couldn't pick cotton like they oughta with you pickin' 'em off with them shot, you crazy dunce you!"

"Know what, Lawrence?" said Filbert as he wiped a string of saliva from his neglected chin of black spines. "Papa says I can't hit nothin' with my 20-gauge. Oh yeah? I sure wish he'd let me take a pop at him 'bout 75 yards away. I sure could check his oil for him."

Struck with amusement by his own words, the bony one cackled out until his father cut him short with: "Gwan an' eat yer supper and quit slobberin' in yer plate."

"That's all right, papa! Least I don't spit in the hall like you do!"

"Shut yer mouth! You jest mad 'cause I can outshoot you."

"Heck you can! You're too dang ol' to shoot straight. All you can kill with 'at 12-gauge o' yours is a mockin' bird once in a while, when you take rest. An' that ain't often. You ruinin' the pecan trees shootin' limbs out from under them birds. God gonna punish you for ruinin' them trees."

"Aw, shut your breakfast...I meant shut yer mouth an' eat yer supper, you crazy dunce you."

"Papa won't even buy me no shells, Lawrence."

"Don't need no shells. By gad, ya got eight or nine in there. How many ya want, anyway?"

"Awright, if that's the way you gonna do, papa, I won't kill no more squirrels. I'll jist let th' suckers eat all yo corn right down to the ground. Now ain't you gonna feel like a swell son-of-a-gun when you come out some mornin' and' find yo whole field lookin' like the bad man done slapped the devil outa the whole place?"

"Ain't but one squirrel on the place, you crazy dunce. I'll git him before harvest time."

"Shucks you will! Yo gun ain't got no power. Them Niggas 'cross the railroad say ever time I shoot they heah me go `Pow!' They can't never heah yo gun, 'less the win's blowin' that way."

"Aw git out with that! Niggas thought there was a war startin' last week when I cut loose on that ol' bull."

"Yeah, but you didn't git nowhere with it. Dang bull jist kept shovin' 'gainst the dang fence til he knocked it down an' went on through like you wasn't nowhere to be seen. Papa, you could shoot better if you got them long eyebrows cut off."

"That ain't got nothin' to do with mah shootin'."

"Heck, it don't. Next time you go to the barber git him to cut them brows like I do. You oughta get 'im to cut them hairs in yo ears, too, so you can heah better. Shucks, I even get 'im to cut the hairs outa my nose. I git mah money's worth."

"I ain't gonna ask no dentist to do nothin' like that, you crazy dunce you."

"I didn't say a dentist. You said a dentist and you meant a barber."

"Pshaw, it don't make no difference."

I would stop the growling of the two men, I thought, by asking the younger one about his melon patch.

"Aw," said Granddo before his son could reply, "that boy don't know how to raise nothin'."

"Heck, I don't! God jist ain't fair to me, that's all. He made th' rain wash up all my cantaloupes and watermelons. Know what I'm gonna do next spring, Lawrence? I'm gonna plant somethin' else 'cept melons. He's gonna be all ready to open up the whole dang sky and wash up my watermelons, and He's sure gonna git fooled when He finds out I ain't got no melons to be washed up. He sure is gonna git fooled!"

Again Niagara Falls in miniature came stringing over a precipice of stained teeth and answered the call of gravity as the bony one giggled fatuously until ired Granddo sobered him with his usual "Gwan and eat yer supper!"

CHAPTER SEVENTEEN

Quivering Nostrils in Filbert's Room

At 8:30 Granddo, realizing that it was past his bedtime, remarked: "Reckon you boys can sleep in the room this side of Filbert's. Reckon we better turn in."

"Ain't that funny why the ol' man thinks we gotta go to bed this early," commented the son, as his parent plumped up the hallway. "He sure is a sight 'bout this sleepin' business. When he goes to bed he thinks I ougtha go to bed. You oughta heah th' crazy ol' fool beatin' on the wall sometimes when I stay up and look at the funny paper. 'Cut out that lamp and go on to bed!' he's always yellin'. Ain't got sense 'nough to 'member we got 'lectric lights now 'stead of lamps. Guess I'm gonna haft to see 'bout having 'im sent down to the feeble-minded home — if he's got sense 'nough to live down there, which I doubt to heck he does."

"Come on in my den," he said with an unapologetic belch. "I'm gonna show you guys somepin."

Kicking aside a heap of socks that reeked strong appeals for laundry service, Filbert stopped before an antique dresser and began to rummage in the drawers.

After more than a little slobbering and fussing, he located the object of his search — a motley shirt of red, yellow, and green.

"How you like my Meskin shirt?" he said, proudly holding up the flashy garment. "Them Niggas sure scared o' me when I wear this thing. You oughta see how them suckers pick cotton when I got this on. I sure do make 'em pull them bolls. Papa says I couldn't be a good boss man. Heck, I couldn't! Bet I'd make them babies look like bird shot rolling up and down them rows. Trouble with papa, he's too ol'. He ain't got no more nerve 'bout him...ain't got guts 'nough to git him a hickory club and rake out a lotta teeth when them babies slow down. Suckers stop work three or four times a day to git water.

"Now ain't that a heck of a mess! Wish we had some Meskins working' heah...or maybe some Indians."

"Think you could handle Indians, McCord?" asked Carl.

"Sure I could...if I had plenty o' shells and a big cowboy hat like Tom Mix got."

"I'll make you a promise," said Carl. "The next time we capture some Indians, we'll tie 'em up, and put 'em in a big crate and send them to you by express. But you be sure you have plenty of ammunition with you when you meet the train."

"You mean you and Lawrence done...aw, there ain't no more Indians loose to be had. Least that's what papa said. Papa said the law done killed all the bad Indians."

"You mean you haven't seen Tom Mix fighting Indians?"

"Yeah, but papa said that ain't really so. He said all 'at picture show business is all a dang lie."

"Oh, but your papa's badly mistaken. Lawrence and I have seen some of the Indian fight pictures being filmed, haven't we, Lawrence?"

"You bet we have."

"McCord, those movie producers sometimes spend thousands of dollars in making a single scene. Naturally, they want these scenes to look real. Now when they want to show a really good and natural Indian fight, they just go out in the desert and pick a fight with a tribe of redskins."

That my relative was a bit skeptical was evident in his "How you know they do?"

"Why, Filbert," said I, "these movie producers make a lot of pictures in the foothills near Mesa and we go up and watch. Sometimes we crouch down in the Ford, drive in among them, and get a few of the redmen ourselves."

"Lots of sport, McCord," said Sharkey. "Just like knocking' off swamp rabbits."

"I sure wish to heck I could git in on some of that! Boy, I sure would give them rascals the devil or my name ain't McCord. Bet you I'd kill more Indians than anybody in the world!

"Lawrence, you gotta take me back with you so I can kill some Indians. Come on now, Lawrence...I'm yo uncle now. You can't be a good Christian 'less you take yo uncle out to pot Indians. Come on now, Lawrence. 'Member that Christmas I give you that ol' sweater that was too big for me? How 'bout it, Lawrence — can I go...huh?"

"We'll see, Fill. We'll see."

"One time," said Carl, "we captured a chief."

"You pot 'im first?"

"No, we laid our guns aside and used our bare hands."

"You mean you didn't even have no club?"

"Nope."

"Well, I ain't ever heard of anything like that. Papa said a man got to have a gun or a club to git a Indian."

"He's mistaken again, my good fellow. Ever hear of the old pittlehollyjack trick?"

"Yeah, seems like my Sunday School teacher, when I was in the fourth grade, tol' me somepin like 'at. But I don't 'member what she said."

"Too bad, my friend. You'll never be much of an Indian hunter unless you learn the uh...the middlehollysock."

This was one time when Sharkey failed to recall correctly one of his impromptu coined names.

"Lawrence," said Filbert turning to me, "you gotta teach me 'at pisselholjunk stuff."

"I'm sorry, Fil, but I'm afraid it's a little too rough for you."

"Yes, it takes a real man," said Carl, "to learn to apply the middlehollyjack."

"You gotta teach me 'at hold, now. Lawrence, if you don't teach me, I'm gonna tell yo mama next time I see her 'at hornet didn't jest happen to light in Aunt Betty's bloomers 'at time she came in her room and put 'em on and broke her ankle. If you think I won't, jest...."

"Okay, show him the hold. Sharkey."

Reading the sparkle of mischief in my buddy's eyes, I looked at the floor and observed that it was rugless. I hoped my skinny relative's bones were not too brittle, for very soon uncle and oak would collide.

For a moment after the collision, the former lay there grunting and looking himself over to determine whether or not he was still in one piece.

Seconds later, after mumbling something about "a shot o' salts," he was gripping his breeches and hurrying to the outside privy.

While the other Beebuzzard rollicked in merriment, I went to my suitcase and secured some materials I had brought along especially for Filbert's "benefit" — a few lumps of ferrous sulfide and a little bottle of diluted sulfuric acid. Exposed to one another, these two substances would produce an odor similar to that contained in cesspools.

"You going to give him the ol' rotten-egg treatment tonight, Left?"

"I'm not about to whip up a love potion, my rumpbumping friend."

When Filbert returned complaining "That's the sixth time tonight," the stench from the concoction concealed under his bed was just beginning to become noticeable.

"I sure did gas the whole dang place up," he suffixed to a pair of sniffs. In a desperate attempt to expel the intensifying smell, he fanned the air with his "Meskin" shirt.

"I ain't never seen nothin' like this!" he puffed. "The mo' I fan, the worse it gits."

At last when the room was almost saturated with stench, Filbert turned fiercely to me with the accusation:

"You guys been helpin' stink up this place! You been eatin' a lotta rotten mess and stinkin' heck outa my room. I oughta knowed it long time ago. Shucks, a dang elephant couldn't fill a little place like this that quick. You guys gonna keep me from sleepin'. I ain't gonna take it, by shucks!"

Acquainted with the raging fury which sometimes possessed my uncle, I quickly bade him goodnight, pushed Carl into our quarters, and quickly shut and bolted the door behind us.

Carl's heehawing and Filbert's condemnation of "them stinkin' polecats" having ended, I lay on a warm mattress and looked southward at a nearby creek and swamp. There a company of nocturnal denizens, relieved that man had retired indoors, had come forth to serenade the moon, the shadows, and the magnolias.

Somewhere along the sluggish waterway, a whonking bullfrog grunted a lazy response to an inquiring hoot owl.

And was that seemingly stuttering whippoorwill in the westerly wood lot really saying, "Make-him-talk, make-him-talk?"

And what were the whispering crickets saying?

I might have decoded their chirpings but for a sudden rough banging that snatched me back from the animal world to the human.

"Dang yo time, Lawrence," said Uncle Filbert, beating the barrel of his shotgun against my bolted door, "you guys done stunk up my den so much I can't stand it! An' papa gonna smell it and try to gimme some castor oil. I ain't gonna take it now!"

"Take it easy, Uncle Filbert," I urged. "It'll make a man out of you."

"I ain't gonna take it now! Jest 'cause you go to college, you think you can make a idiot outa me an' stink up my den. Papa gonna think my guts is all rotten!"

"We're sorry, Fil" was my assurance.

"I'm gonna come in there and check yo oil with this 20-gauge, by shucks!"

"Filbert," said I, as I stuffed a newspaper under the door to keep out the leaking-in odor, "if you want us to take you back with us to pot some Indians, you'll calm down right now!"

My ultimatum seemed to effect speedy results, for Filbert propped his gun in a corner and again began his fast fanning.

"I sure hope papa don't smell this stuff," he gasped during a rest period. He coughed a bit, blew his nose, and began grumbling to himself.

And then suddenly he went on another rampage.

"To heck with pottin' 'em Indians," he stormed. "You guys hep me git this mess out o' mah room, or I'm gonna shoot heck outa you suckers!"

His outburst and threats came to an abrupt end, however, when a fist pounded loudly against a wall adjoining his room and a voice boomed out: "You crazy dunce, if you don't quit having' them fool nightmares, I'm gonna haft to put you back in that feeble-minded home!"

CHAPTER EIGHTEEN

White Strand in the Bacon

"Atta boy, Filbert, shoot 'im again!" I yelled two days later as I watched my uncle fire a fifth time at a dead squirrel we Beebuzzards previously had placed surreptitiously in a nearby walnut tree.

Likewise enjoying the show, Sharkey encouraged the hunter with: "You wounded him that time! Next shot oughta bring him down. Get the lead out, McCord, and we'll have squirrel for dinner!"

Another report. Another expression of disgust. Another reloading.

"Just like July the Fourth in June!" chuckled Sharkey.

But when a seventh load of shot hit the mangled rodent, it left its retinue of green flies and fell near the shotgunist's feet.

"I knowed you couldn't get away!" squealed Filbert. "Shucks, I was too smart for you!"

A moment later we joined him and offered our congratulations.

"Excellent demonstration of marksmanship, ol' fellow," complimented Carl. "You shot only seven times! Excellent hunting, simply excellent!"

"Fil," said I, "you're a real McCord. Yes sir, only a McCord could have killed that squirrel so easily and skillfully. I'm proud that you're my uncle and that I'm your nephew!"

"But," I added in another tone, "I'm very much ashamed that you have killed a female squirrel at this season of the year."

"Well," said Carl, "I didn't realize until now you were so cruel and heartless. How could you murder a mother and leave helpless little ones in a nest to starve to death? The Humane Society should be informed about this barbarous misdeed."

Filbert's chest had grown smaller, his mouth wider. His eyes hadn't decided yet what course to take.

"But dang it all," he protested finally, "how'n heck could I see it was a mama squirrel? I ain't got no field glasses on!"

"But thunderation, McCord, you weren't more than 60 feet from the animal. A mole with the pink eye could have seen it was a female."

"Yeah, but I ain't no mole, Lewis!"

Amused at his own inadvertently humorous retort, the "sharp-shooter" traded his mood of indignation for a fling at laughter. The sound of his own giggles amused him all the more, and eventually he was virtually howling in glee.

"Wist I was in a circus," he managed to say between convulsions, "I'd make everybody laugh his guts out." Emitting even greater peals of hilarity, he dropped his gun and embraced the trunk of the tree for support.

I let him unwind himself a bit more and then brought him to sobriety with: "I despise having to do it, Uncle Filbert, but I feel it my duty as a Christian and an American citizen to report this out-of-season killing to a game warden."

Had I not been holding our victim's gun, I wouldn't have risked arousing his volative temper.

"Yeah, an' I'm gonna tell 'bout them bloomers, Lawrence. You think I won't? I'm gonna tell, even if I don't git to pot no Indians, by shucks!"

"Too bad, McCord, and you looked like a fine, law-abiding citizen. You had me fooled, ol' man. When and how did you get off on such a criminal career? Don't you want to tell us about it — get it all off your chest? Come on, ol' fella, make a clean confession of all the misdeeds you've committed and you'll feel much better. You'll find us just as sympathetic and kind as two human beings can be — under the circumstances. We've got to turn you in, of course, but on the way to jail we'll give you the best in the way of legal advice and...."

"I ain't goin' to jail, now dang it!"

"Easy now, Uncle Filbert. You won't have to cook eggs and wash dishes while you're in jail. Think of it—you won't have anything to do...nothing but sleep and rest."

"Yeah, an' nothin' to eat but ol' hard beans and bread. I hear papa tell 'bout 'at jail business. I might haft to beat up rocks with a hammer. I ain't gonna go, Lawrence, I ain't gonna go! An' you ain't got to tell nobody 'bout 'at squirrel now!"

"It won't be so bad, McCord," consoled Carl. "We'll send you some chewing tobacco for Christmas and maybe something on your birth-day, and we'll be by to see you sometime next summer. Why, thunderation, man, it ought to be a sort of vacation for you!"

"Yeah, an' what would papa do out heah all by hisself an' nobody to fix his eggs and wash dishes? Pore ol' sucker would git starved and die dead sure as the devil!"

"Now, McCord, you needn't worry about that. We'll have your father sent to a home for old folks where he'll be taken care of, you can be sure."

"Heck you will! Gimme 'at gun, Lawrence! I'm gonna check heck outa somebody's oil. Ain't nobody gonna send mah papa to a ol' folks home!"

We would now have to subdue my thin relative without injuring him.

We had him panting and his shoulders on the ground when an intruding voice boomed nearby, "What's goin' on heahabouts?"

"Oh, we're just showing Filbert an Indian hold, Granddo," I replied after an awkward hesitation.

"Papa, they're gonna send...." Filbert's intended accusation ended in shrill laughter.

Hurrah for Sharkey! His quick tickling Filbert's very sensitive ribs prompted the mustachioed parent to say, "That boy's kinda enjoyin' that tusslin'!"

Granddo's withdrawal, more guffaws sprinkled with slang, the sounds of a horn and the closing of a car door. Then came Granddo's shout: "It's Boyd, and that gull from way out yonder! You boys quit yer tusslin' and come on to the house!"

Free and cloaked in dirt, Filbert leaped from his berth on the ground and ran to greet cousin Boyd and his hefty wife Julia "from way out yonder" in the West.

"How's my Filly Boy gittin' along?" Julia asked, after she had aimed a kiss at his cheek, missed, and caught him on the ridge of his nose.

"Them guys gonna tell on me an' put papa in...."

"How're you, Cousin Julia?" I inquired just in time.

She was glad to see me and Carl; she relayed a message from my mother: "Don't be playing tricks on Filbert!"

Next it was time to knuckle-crack Cousin Boyd's hand and have him tell me again, "I'm in bad shape, son. It's them blamed insides of mine."

He was going into the third phase of his health report when his overshadowing spouse cut him off with: "Boss, git Filly Boy that cactus candy I brung him from Mesa outa the car."

"You got me some candy from way out yonder, Coz Julie? Bet you them Meskins made it, didn't they? By shucks, I bet you 'at Meskin candy sure will make me tough as a wart on a goat udder."

"That boy don't need no candy," said Granddo. "Gad, he had some last week! What does he need some mo' for?"

Eventually Cousin Julia went to the kitchen to prepare dinner, leaving us to hear about the exploits of the McCords.

Granddo led the round table bragging with a description of his intimidating "a coupla ol' Niggas that stole a bitch bird dog from mah chicken yard."

Filbert told how he had frightened, at the point of his shotgun, "Mista William's kid way from fishin' in papa's fish pond!"

And Cousin Boyd re-enacted a scene starring himself standing fearless before a customer who had complained that he must have been incapable of reading since he had failed to carry out her written instructions directing him to press, not clean, her husband's pants.

"Madam," he had said to her, "did you think up all that brilliant sarcasm by yourself? Now aren't you smart! I guess you don't ever make an error yoreself. Huh? Madam, how does it feel to be perfect? You must get mighty lonely without any company — just you and God!"

Granddo laughed because he felt that the tailor expected him to laugh. Filbert laughed because he thought he would reveal himself a fool who could not grasp a funny story unless he did laugh. And we Beebuzzards laughed at the three of them for reasons apparent.

We were moving down the corridor in response to the dinner bell when Cousin Boyd whispered, "You boys played any tricks on Filbert yet?"

For the sake of self defense, I was about to give him a negative reply when he said, "Julia would skin me alive if she saw the big artificial bullfrog I bought to fool him with. You know how he likes to hunt them things."

Granddo must have been rather thankful today, for his blessing was longer than usual. He had speeded up his tempo and was sprinting down the last stretch when Cousin Boyd, who could no longer tolerate the tickling in his throat, whipped out his brandy flask and took a hasty nip.

He had hoped it would go unobserved, but Cousin Julia saw him and dug an elbow into his stomach, unintentionally pumping out a noise that was a half cough and half grunt.

To utter a quick amen and thereby end grace-saying at an unexpected point was an old trick Granddo had learned to use to good advantage during the days when debate at the McCord table was a favorite sport among the family males. This artifice, now merely a hangover from the yesteryears, had made it possible for him to plunge immediately into his side of an argument before the other participants had even an opportunity to lift their heads from their plates.

Determined not to be outdone again, I tuned my neck almost in unison with his, and before the others realized fully that the blessing had ended, I had passed the bacon to Filbert and Granddo had commented, "Stuff looks kinda good."

"I could cook a good dinner, too, papa," said my uncle, "if I had a good watch."

"Don't need no watch, you crazy dunce you. Gad, we got a time piece in the hall. Don't need no mo'. If you jest got to have a time piece, git you a Karo lid an' a spool an' make you a sun dial."

"Now wouldn't I play the devil tryin' to time them eggs with a fool sun dial?"

"You can't cook nothin' 'ceptin' eggs an' taters."

"The shucks I can't! I made some candy one time and...."

Another subject took Filbert's attention. It was a long white hair which undoubtedly had grown weary of Cousin Julia and had sought the company of younger meat, namely the bacon in my uncle's plate.

"Now ain't that somepin!" fumed Filbert, as he held the greasy strand aloft for the scrutiny of all and the discomfiture of my female cousin.

"Gwan and eat yer stuff there?" commanded Granddo.

"I ain't got no appetite now, not after I...."

"You jest eat too much of them mesquite sweets," said Granddo.

"You mean cactus candy, you crazy ol' fool."

"Don't make no difference what it was! Gwan an' shut your stuff...I mean your mouth and eat yer dinner."

"Now how'n heck am I gonna shut mah mouth an' eat? A man gotta have his mouth open to git his food in."

"You ought to break yourself from that slang habit, Filbert" was Cousin Boyd's indirect reproval.

"I tried two or three times to stop, Coz Boyd, but papa says 'em so much I can't quit."

"The heck I do!" snapped Granddo. "Don't do no such a danged thing."

"Now, Boss," said Cousin Julia to her henpecked mate, "jest you leave Filly Boy alone and tend to yore own faults. Leastwise, he don't go 'round hanging on to no brandy bottle."

"Madam, I've told you a thousand times, if I've told you once! Dr. Hogue said drink it for my throat. It kills the germs."

Sharkey had to meddle with: "That's not all it will kill."

"What did you say, son?"

"I said it's just like a pill."

"That's what I thought you said."

"Coz Boyd," said Filbert, "bet you if you was to drink some of mah coffee you wouldn't haft to drink no more alkeehol."

"Gad, that stuff that boy makes is too danged strong," put in Granddo.

"Well, shucks, papa, that's the way I want it so I can stay up an' listen to Brother Hill through my radio. You think I wanta go to sleep on the job and go to hell? Papa, for shucks sake git 'at nasty ol' buttermilk outa yo beard. You tryin' to make mah stomick git all messed up?"

"Don't make you any sicker than them black whiskers o' yours make me, you crazy dunce you. When you gonna shave? You ain't shave in three or four days."

"Christ never did shave, you crazy ol' fool? You think you're better'n Christ? Me an' Him jest alike — we ain't got time to shave, an' it cost money to all time be usin' blades. You don't gimme...Coz Julie, papa done cut me down to two bits a week."

"Why, Tom McCord! How do you expect the pore boy to git along on 25 cents a week?"

"He don't need no mo'," growled Granddo as he stuck his fork into a jar of fig preserves.

"There he goes," said Filbert, "putting' his fork in them figs. Don't you see 'at spoon, papa? Use 'at spoon. Nobody wants to eat after you an' 'at dirty ol' beard you got."

"I think Filly Boy oughta git at least four bits a week, Tom," opined our hair-shedding cook.

"Now, Madam," interposed Cousin Boyd, "I reckon Tom knows what the boy needs. Let's leave...."

"I don't care what you reckon, Boss!" shrilled the suddenly vexed wife. "You keep yore snout outa this. I'm talkin' business to Tom. Now, Tom, don't you think yore own flesh and blood oughta git more than two bits a week?"

"Susie...I mean Julia, I ain't gonna let that boy ruin himself on no four bits a week...'fraid he might throw hisself away on foolishness. But I'll try 'im on 35 cents awhile and see how he behaves hisself."

"Yippee! You hear papa, Lawrence? He gonna gimme a raise...gonna gimme 35 cents!" Filbert's enthusiasm was genuine. He was really excited and pleased that his seven-day allotment was to assume a 10-cent increase.

"Let me be the first to congratulate you," said Sharkey.

Although my uncle cried out in pain, my fellow Beebuzzard squeezed the former's knuckles long enough to overturn a bowl of gravy in his victim's lap.

"Now look what you done did!" screamed Filbert as he reached for a cup towel with which to remove the dripping sauce.

"Now, Filly Boy, it was an accident," soothed Cousin Julia, rising to assist in the mopping of his overalls. "And I really think it was yore own hand that knocked the bowl over."

"That boy chews too much tobacco," put in Granddo. "His hand shakes too much."

"Yeah, but anybody's hand gonna shake," defended 'that boy,' "if somebody got hold of it and wiggled the devil out of it!"

"Aw, gwan an' eat yer supper and quit that slobberin' in yer plate, you crazy dunce you."

"Don't you know this ain't supper, papa? You mean dinner. If you don't quit callin' things by the wrong names, we gonna haft to put you down in the feeble-minded home, you crazy ol' fool!"

CHAPTER NINETEEN

Sanctuary in the Swamp

"Better change yer mind an' come along, Boyd," said Granddo as he harnessed a pair of tail-swishing mules to his aged wagon Saturday morning. "Niggas will all be comin' to their houses with money in their pockets. Won't take me long to sell 'em all these beans. Then I'll git mah bucket of coffee and sugar, an' we'll head fer home. Oughta git back by sundown."

"Yeah, thas what you said, papa, the time them dang mules ran away an' busted blazes outa some spokes in one of them front wheels. We didn't git back to the farm til 'bout midnight. You too ol' and weak-minded to drive a wagon."

"Ain't no such a thing, you crazy dunce you. It was that otha fella that caused that trouble. Crazy fool blowed his whistle an' bumped over Nancy's hoof at the same time. Musta been a danged yankee drivin' that buggy."

"That wasn't no buggy! It was a car!"

"Don't make no different 'bout that. How 'bout it, Boyd, you comin' or not?"

"I sure would like to, Tom, but I guess I'd better stay here and try to get them blamed inside o' mine to loosen up."

"You boys care 'bout goin'?" This to us from Granddo.

"Thanks, Granddo," I replied, looking up from my whittling on a bean shooter stalk, "but we've got something we want to do here on the place."

"Boss!" a voice called from the farm kitchen.

"Yes, Madam!" Cousin Boyd was quick to answer.

"You come on in here, Boss, and hep me can these beans for Tom. Him and Filly Boy will need all they can git this winter."

"I'm comin', Madam!"

Filbert, who had been looking at some old newspapers his father was to use in sacking his produce, scowled in disgust at a headline: "Fight in House of Lords."

"Now ain't that a heck of a mess," he said. "Son-of-a-guns fightin' in church. Lewis, you ever seen a fight in a church?"

"No, I can't recall having observed any display of pugnacious activity, aside from an occasional verbal conflict which allegedly proceeded from altruism rather than personal aggrandizement or avariciousness."

"You ain't, I guess. Huh? I ain't neither, but one time I sure thought two guys was gonna have it. They was both tryin' to see who could pray louder'n the other, it seemed to me. You oughta heard them guys. The guy that couldn't pray loud as the other guy told me he wasn't gonna go to that place no mo'. I ain't goin' there, either. They sing too fast for me. I'd go to hell sure at that church, 'cause I never could keep up. Bet you I could keep up, if I could read fast like I could when I was in the fourth grade though."

As if he were treading on holy ground, "Uncle" Mack, one of Granddo's Negro farm hands, hat in hand, approached my grandfather and sought audience by meekly clearing his throat.

"Why ain't you out there weedin' that corn, Nigga?" the employer wanted to know.

"Mista Tom, Ah done teetered down heah fast as mah ol' bunions done let me to ast if you mind gittin' me a can o' snuff in town."

"You don't need no mo'. Got you some last month. What you need some mo' for?"

"Yassuh."

"Yassuh what, Nigga?"

"Yas suh. I guess Ah don' need no mo' — if you say I don'."

"Git on back to the field, Nigga. You know I'll git yo tobacco — if you gotta have it."

"Please, suh, it's snuff Ah wants, stead o' 'bacco."

"I said I'd git yo stuff now. Now git on back to yo work."

"Papa can't git nothin' right," said Filbert to us Beebuzzards. "Ain't no tellin' what the crazy ol' fool gonna git 'at Nigga. One time 'stead of gittin' snuff like he was ast to git, he come back with a box of matches. Now wouldn't 'at Nigga play the devil puttin' matches up his nose?"

"Niggas sure do waste money for foolishness," Granddo regretted as he half drowned a beetle with a spittle of chewing tobacco. "Must be them danged Republicans that got 'em that way."

"Lawrence," said my uncle, "you watch how I can boss Niggas," and to the retreating black man he shouted: "Hey, Uncle Mack, you be sure to hoe them rows cleaner than I know you are! You hear me?"

"Yassuh!"

"Lawrence, you hear 'at Nigga say `suh' to me? He knows I can shoot a 20-gauge. Watch me make him say it again."

"Shut ya mouth and hep me with these traces," demanded Granddo.

"Papa, why you got to stop me every time I'm havin' a good time? You must be 'fraid I'm gonna show people I'm a better boss man than you are."

"You ain't no such a danged thing, you crazy dunce you? Don't you know them Niggas know I can shoot a rifle? Gad, when I was yo age I could shoot a spool o' thread outa a Nigga's mouth at 65 yards. Tried it once. Niggas had so much confidence in mah shootin' they always said I shot the Nigga's tooth out on purpose."

"You pay the doctor bill, papa?"

"He didn't need no doctor. Got mah wife to put some coal oil on it and sent 'im back to the field."

"Dang yo time?" Filbert railed at one of the mules that had laid her tail across his cheek. "I ain't no horsefly!"

The animals fully harnessed, Granddo remembered he had forgotten his pocketbook and returned to his bedroom.

Reassuming his position on the wagon, Filbert addressed me with: "You know if any o' them Indians ever shoot mah teeth out, hope I can git Dr. Ayre to fix me up. You know why I like him, Lawrence? He don't charge me nothin', and when he don't do me no good, I don't lose much."

"Uncle Filbert," said I, "someday I'm going to make you a character in a book I intend to write about the Beebuzzards."

"You mean write about me so everybody in the world will now what a good shot I am?"

"Exactly. Suppose I do write about you and the book brings me some money — how'd you like for me to buy you an automatic 20-gauge?"

"Shucks, I'll be too ol' to shoot a gun by the time you make some money on a book. You don't know nothin' 'bout makin' money. All you know 'bout is goin' to college and foolishness. Why don't you learn to raise corn and be...."

"Lefty might write and sell a book, sure enough, McCord," said Carl. "And if he does, the book might become adapted to the screen and you might be signed by some movie company to play your own part in the picture."

"Is 'at a fact, Lewis? Is 'at right, Lawrence?"

Our answers were, of course, in the affirmative.

"See that long, wide pasture land across the creek, McCord?" asked Carl.

"Why, sure. I ain't gone blind."

"McCord, it's entirely possible that one of these days a big airplane will land there and a big movie producer with a big cigar will get out and say to you, 'I'm looking for Mr. McCord — Mr. Filbert McCord. I've got a 20,000-dollar movie contract I hope to have him sign.' "

"Hot corn and shucking, Lawrence!" exclaimed my excited relative. "You hear that?"

"What would you do with that money, Filbert?" I inquired.

"I'd git me a pony and a big cowboy hat and a pistol and I'd ride up and down town 'til all them Niggas 'at come to town got scared and hollered and said, 'Les git home, for Laud's sakes while we still got our skins on!' An' people would all crowd round an' whoop an' holler an' point at me an' say, 'There goes Mr. Filbert McCord. He done been in a movin' pitcher show.' Bet you they'd try to git me to write mah name on some paper like them real actors do, too."

"What would you say when they called on you to make a speech, Uncle Filbert?"

"I sure would give 'em the best speakin' they ever heard. I'd say: 'Ladies an' gentlemen, I'm here today to tell you that before I joined up with the pitcher show company I was jest a dang fool like you are. I didn't know nothin', cept 'bout shootin' a gun. An' I'm here to tell you that I still know a lot 'bout shootin'...yeah, more'n mah papa does, 'cause he ain't never potted no Indians like me an' Lawrence an' Lewis has. You think...."

Applause from the Beebuzzards and the 40,000 interrupted the "movie idol."

"My good friends," he said in resuming, "I got somepin important to tell you. Sometimes there's gonna be a big war, so you all better git all the shells you can an' practice shootin', 'cause we gonna haft to fight somebody — I don't know who.

"Anybody 'at wants me to show 'em how to load a gun an' git in a marchin' line see me an' I'll show you how. But I'm here to tell you, ain't no need to ast mah papa, 'cause his ideas are all dead. Papa can't boss a Nigga — can't even shoot a gun. He's too ol' an' feeble-minded."

"Ain't no such a danged thing!" thundered Granddo, almost upon us before we noticed his return. And then, just as quickly as he had made his approach, he retreated to the porch, promising angrily, "I'm gonna show you boys somethin' when I git back with mah gun!"

"Honest, papa, I was jest jokin'!" Filbert appealed. "I was jest makin' foolishness!"

"McCord," said Sharkey to my whimpering uncle, "seems to me that you're going to have your oil checked."

"Heck I am!" exclaimed Filbert as he ran for the nearest substantial place of hiding, a dense scuppernong vine.

"Watch out for those big wasp nests under there, Uncle Filbert!" I cautioned, watching him fight his way into a network of greenery.

"Lefty," rebuked Sharkey, "are you forgetting you're a Beebuzzard? Why didn't you let him find those wasps for himself?"

"I would, if there were any, but there aren't; I was under looking at the grape prospects just yesterday."

Bloody-eyed Granddo, coming out with a 12 gauge almost as long as he was tall, looked about and asked gruffly, "Where'd that boy go?"

"He got the idea you were going to shoot him, so he ran, Mr. McCord."

"A boy like that ain't got sense 'nough to handle no 35 cents a week."

"Charles!" he shouted. "Charles, I ain't gonna shoot you, you crazy dunce you? Come on back heah! Come on back heah, I say!"

"Charles," however, remained in quiet concealment.

Sole response to the shouting came from Cousin Julia, who appeared at a window to ask, "For goodness sakes what's goin' on out there, Tom!"

"Ain't nothin', nothin', I say" was the old man's irritated reply. "I'm jest gonna try out mah gun."

Convinced that he was not going "to try it out on Filly Boy," Julia rejoined "Boss" and her beans, leaving Granddo to say, "Well, suh, I said I was gonna show you somethin' an' I'm gonna keep mah word. Now you jest find me a bird, an' I'll show you some shootin'. Now where's a bird?"

"I saw one in the scuppernongs a few minutes ago, Mr. McCord. Looked like a cuckoo bird to me."

"Ain't no such a bird like that 'round heah."

"Why, Mr. McCord. I've seen two every day we've been here, an old one and a young one."

"Ain't none on the place, I say. If you seen a bird in them scuppernongs, musta been a oriole. Ain't but one on the place, but we'll git closer an' see if that's him."

Confident that we were still too far away for Filbert to understand our conversation, I halted our party with: "The bird Carl saw must have gone. Why don't you get your gun in position, Granddo, through that wire fence, and show us how you would aim, if that were an oriole in that tree limb above the scuppernongs?"

"What you want me to do that for?"

"Well, Carl doesn't know much about guns, Granddo, and I'd like for you to show him the best way a man ought to take aim."

"Pshaw, I thought everybody knowed that. Well, now, say I was gonna blast blazes outa a bird out there. I'd git down on one knee like this, point mah barrel like this heah, put mah cheek down like...."

"Papa, for God's sake, I was jest jokin'! Honest! You can boss Niggas an' you got mo' sense...papa, I love you...."

As if struck by a midget twister, the farther end of the scuppernong vine parted to emit clawing, frightened Uncle Filbert, a long-legged structure who believed that his Creator had endowed him with two lower extremities for use in circumstances similar to these.

"Come back heah, you crazy dunce you!"

"Lawrence, your relative doesn't run very long in one spot, does he?" snickered Carl.

"Ain't no need for me to try an' git that boy to come back," concluded my grandfather. "Guess I'll haft to git that gull...what's her name?"

"Cousin Julia?"

"Yeah. Guess I'll haft to git her to put on some boots and go after that boy before he gits snakebit down in that swamp. He won't believe nobody else, I guess."

"Look, Granddo, look at that woodpecker on that mulberry limb! Knock him off and show Carl what a good shot you are."

By the time his target had encircled the limb, Granddo had rested his shotgun barrel on the fence and was trying to draw a fine bead, as if he were aiming a rifle at a small object at least 100 yards distant.

"That's the trouble with a danged pecker," he grumbled, "they jest too danged nervous. Acts like somebody was gonna hurt 'im, the crazy dunce!"

Suddenly his left shoulder, as if it had abruptly become morbidly frightened, seemed trying to hide behind his chest...his eyes showed difficulty in pursuing his head...and, in general, he was a battered and backward moving little man. He had just pulled the trigger on his big 12-gauge.

Apparently unharmed, Inspector Woodpecker postponed his tour of the mulberry until a later date and rocketed away toward the land where all scared folk in this region seemed to seek sanctuary — the swamp.

"You didn't miss everything, Mr. McCord," said Carl, "you got a coupla leaves."

"He got more than that, Sharkey!" I asserted, as if I were offended that he should fail to give my grandfather all the credit due him. "He knocked down one or two green mulberries, and they were mighty close to that bird...not much more than ten or twelve inches from it, by golly!"

And what did the little marksman have to say?

"It's them dadblamed sorry shells they been sellin' for the last 15 years! They ain't puttin' 'nough powder in them blame things...ain't givin' me mah money's worth. Reckon them danged Republicans musta taken over the whole ammunition works, too!"

CHAPTER TWENTY

Breeches at Half Mast

Self-reliance was a quality Granddo evidently liked to exercise sometimes to extremeness. Today, for instant, he had declined Cousin Boyd's offer to take him and Filbert to "Sunday meetin' " in his sedan, and he likewise turned down a chance to jingle in The Carcass.

"Nont," he had grunted, "ain't no need for you to waste yo gas an' oil in haulin' us. Me an' that boy'll jest straddle the mules, as usual, an' git there in plenty time."

" 'At stuff may be awright with you, papa, 'cause you got a saddle, but I ain't got nothin' but a dang ol' wore-out blanket 'tween 'at jackass an' me" had been a protest in vain.

And so father and son, bolstered by the morale support of the Beebuzzards and the 40,000, were now engaged in the task of grooming their mounts for the journey to come.

"I'll be dang, papa, looks like...."

"Shut yer mouth on them slang words," growled Granddo. "Today's the Lord's day."

"Yeah, but how 'bout you, papa? You say 'em all time on the Lord's day."

"Don't do no such a danged thing! Now git to puttin' a bridle on that animal."

Hoofs stomped in protest against hit-and-run insects, big bellies rumbled grumbles about too much corn consumptions, and big mouths chomped hostilely on rattling bits.

"Papa, mah chassis jest ain't made for 'at ol' mule. Besides, mah skin's tender. I git rheumatism every time we go to meetin'. Why'n heck can't we go in the wagon?"

"Don't look jest right to be comin' to meetin' in no wagon" was Granddo's explanation. "Makes us look like we got some stuff to peddle, like we did yesterday. And it ain't right to make the animals carry that extry load on the Lord's day."

"Yeah, but them Tolberts and some mo' people come in wagons."

"Don't make no difference 'bout that. I ain't gonna trespass 'cause they do."

A nudge and a gesture from Carl called my attention to Cousin Boyd, who was approaching from the house. Having installed a little surprise for him to encounter in the outside toilet, a stone's throw from our position in the hitching stable, we hoped that his coming our way was but a detour and that he would soon turn back to the trail leading to that little nook behind the cow shed.

"Tom," said he to Granddo, "you better reconsider and let me drive you over in the jitney."

"Nont, we'll git there all right, and it won't cost nobody nothin'."

"But, papa, how 'bout all the time it gonna take them mules to git there?"

"Pshaw, what's time to a mule, you crazy dunce you?"

"Lewis," said Filbert, hoping that an outsider might influence his father to reconsider, whereas he and Cousin Boyd had failed, "it sure is a long ways me an' papa got to go on these jennies."

"Ain't no such a danged thing! Ain't no mo' than five miles from the pasture gate."

Noting Cousin Boyd's increasing fidgeting, Filbert said, "You still havin' trouble with them insides lockin' on you?"

"I sure am, Filbert. Fact is, I'm on my way to the Johnny now to see if I can't get some action of some kind."

"Well, by shucks, you oughta jolt 'long on one o' these rough jackasses ten miles like me an' papa gonna do. Bet you mah Meskin shirt 'gainst them unbuttoned pants you got on, them jackasses sure would make you unload. You oughta see how ridin' them scamps shakes hair outa mah head. Time I get to be a deacon, I ain't gonna have no hair, an' it's gonna be papa's fault, too."

"Them animals ain't makin' you lose no hair, you crazy dunce you. You jest got mange. Told you 'bout hangin' 'round them Niggas' hounds. Yer hair wouldn't come out so much, if you'd git it cut off short."

"Yeah, if I listened to you, I'd git the whole mess shaved off. Now wouldn't I make the bad man laugh with mah head shaved an' stickin' up through mah hair I didn't have no mo'! You jest tryin' to make me git crazy lookin' so they'll 'point you a deacon 'stead o' me. I know you, papa!"

"Look at that sorry stuff, Boyd," said Granddo. "He had found a split in one of the bridle straps. "Now I got that thing down at that fella's place ain't been ten year, an' it's tryin' to play out already. Can't git nothin' any count now days. Danged Republicans got their hands in everythin', I reckon. Don't do no good to vote 'em out of office, 'cause they git in everythin', anyway."

"Papa, who you gonna vote for sheriff next time?"

"I don't know offhand. Reckon it'll be that fella."

"What fella you talkin' 'bout?"

"That fella...you know that fella I'm talkin 'bout!"

The shotgun scare of yesterday was still vivid in Filbert's memory, and so he forbore calling his parent the usual "crazy ol' fool" for failing to remember a name. Instead, he suggested, "You must mean John Butter."

"Don't no such a thing! I'm talkin' 'bout that fella with that place over yonder." Granddo made a sweeping gesture that could have been indicating any place eastward. Then he became comparatively definite.

"You crazy dunce you," he roared, "I mean that fella that's got that place in town!"

Since there were but two candidates in the sheriff race, Filbert's second guess was correct.

"I'd like to vote for him, too, papa, but he gonna lose an', by heck, I ain't gonna vote for no man that ain't gonna win."

"Fil," said I, "do you really vote at election time?"

"Why, shucks yes! Why you think I ain't spose to vote? I ain't no Nigga. Them Niggas sure do wist they was me when one o' them guys in town come out in a big car an' gimme a cigar an' take me in on 'lection day to vote."

The mention of cigars reminded my grandfather that he had a pair in his shirt pocket. One he inserted in his mouth, the other he offered to my cousin.

"Thanks, but I jest put in a fresh wad," declined the latter.

"I ain't had no cigar give me in a long time," hinted Filbert, and Granddo responded with: "Heah, take this comb and git the mud outa that animal's hide."

"Yeah, but if I had a smoke I could pull harder, papa."

"You don't need no cigar. Gad, you had one last week. What you want with some mo' for?"

"I wouldn't care 'bout one, papa, 'cept I could work better with this comb, if I had one. Dang it, I ain't had no strength in mah hands since you got that oil stove and got rid of the wood stove. I sure wist we had that stove back so I could stay strong carryin' in wood. Today's Father's Day, papa...you oughta gimme 'at cigar."

"Don't make no difference 'bout that — you ain't no parent, you crazy dunce you!"

"Yeah, but you are, an' papas spose to give their kids somepin on Father's Day so the kids gonna 'member their papas."

My uncle slobbered a grin that came to an end when Granddo said, "Heah, gimme that comb, if you ain't man enough to use it. Now go git some water for these animals."

"Now that is jest the reason I ain't got no gitup. Totin' water all time done took all my strength. How 'bout 'at smoke, papa?"

"Gwan an' shut yer mouth now an' behave yerself an' I'll give you th' smoke after we git back. Ain't gonna take chances on you gittin' sick an' fallin' out on the meetin' house floor like you did one time I give you a smoke.

"Yeah, but I was jest a kid then."

"You ain't much more'n a kid now."

"Papa, for shucks sake, why you all time sayin' 'at? I'm gonna be 34 mah next birthday."

"Don't make no difference 'bout that. Gwan an' git that water!"

Finally the two mounted their mules, Granddo shouted his assurance that they'd "be home for dinner 'round two o'clock," and then they jolted away. Tall Filbert was fretting and sitting on his hand to relieve his "mis'ry" and short Granddo was tossing stiffly up and down, holding his head high as if he were an emperor on a royal stallion.

A moment later when Cousin Boyd reached his original destination and squeaked the door shut on the catalogued "Johnny," we took our posts behind it. There I renewed my thanksgiving that we had let him be the leader in the artificial frog prank. Uncle Filbert had wasted two shells in an effort to "kil 'at goggle-eyed sucker," half hidden by swamp brush. We could now work Cousin Boyd over thoroughly without fear that he would offer too much complaint, for one word from us to Cousin Julia about her mate's role in that prank and life for Boss would not be too pleasant for awhile.

But if this project worked out according to our expectations, we would not need to remind the locked one that good sportsmanship was preferable to the wrath of the Madam, for he was not expected ever to know that his rump had received a charge from our little hand generator.

How careful we had been to make sure the points of the two tiny nails which were to convey the stimulating current did not rise above the shadowy oval on which our victim was to seat himself. "Victim" did I say? Let us more appropriately refer to him as the "patient." For, after all, were we not seeking to give him the therapeutic "action" he sought? Considering that the Beebuzzards were really intent on serving my kinsman by shocking the devil and everything else out of him, wouldn't it be a noble gesture on the part of you, kind reader, if you were to think of this not as a malodorous outhouse but a clinic where the patient was to be treated by Dr. Lewis and Dr. Nelson?

And those green creatures buzzing about — they weren't flies, but internees.

And that voice in the distance. To whom did it belong? The head nurse? And what was the head nurse screaming?: "Boss, hurry up and git your business done out there and hep me dress them ducks for dinner!"

"Now, Madam," the patient responded, "this business takes time! I'm still tryin' to get some action of some kind!"

"Dr. Lewis," said I, "the patient is desirous of action.

"Then get the lead out and give it to him," returned my fellow medic.

"Let's reverse the phraseology, Dr. Lewis, and say: 'Give it to him and get the lead out.' Wouldn't you like to administer this treatment?"

"The patient is yours. I'll hold the generator and you let fly with all you've got, Doctor Nelson."

"In view of the fact that you did most of the wiring, I think that the privilege of doing this service should be yours."

"Good turn' is more like it. Be sure you give it a good, stiff turn. Remember, he'll be off the 'table' after the first twist, so make it a hardy one, Doc."

"Dr. Lewis," I said, "let's get a little closer so we can experience a better hearing."

As we tiptoed nearer the medley of grunts, mutterings, and blustering within, my associate breathed the warning that "We'd better hurry before the head nurse calls again and gets him off his perch to the clinic kitchen."

He had hardly finished speaking when the feminine voice called out again: "Now, Boss, jest give it up for this morning and come on in here! You can try it again this afternoon."

"All right, Madam!"

"Quick, Lefty, give it a twist!"

Not until that moment had I realized how much could be wrought by a simple twist of the wrist, and not until then had I realized how really emotional were the McCords.

Lurching forward like an Eskimo going to a whale fry and howling as if he had just attempted an enema with a radium-plated syringe, he came bounding out, his trousers hanging down below his knees and tripping him as he ran.

"For goodness sakes, Boss!" exclaimed his wife from the kitchen window. "I didn't mean for you to hurry like...Boss, for sakes alive, have you gone slap dab crazy? Don't stand there coughin' and lookin' like a idiot. Pull up yore breeches an' tell me what's the matter with you!"

And when Boss continued to cough and look at himself, trying to ascertain the injury done to his hind quarters, she shrilled anew with "Git yore breeches up, Boss, before I come out there an' snatch out what little hair you got left."

"Madam," Boss managed to say finally, "I'm afraid you're gonna have a mighty sick man on your hands. I've been stung half to death by yellow jacks, an' I've done swallowed my wad to boot."

CHAPTER TWENTY-ONE

The Pajama Agreement

Today, three mornings after Cousin Boyd had thanked us for "riddin' the closet of them blamed yellow jacks," we chugged into a Baptist revival encampment which Cousin Julia had made us promise we would visit en route back to Mesa.

The camp, peaceful among cooing doves and lowing beeves, extended over a series of grassy hills studded with small mountain oaks, tents, and a few cabins. Looking down from the highest of these hills, we saw other man-made stand-outs. These were an administration building, a mess hall, and the tabernacle.

Because the huge boulder near which we pitched our rustic tent resembled a magnifying glass, we elected to name our camping spot "The Monocle."

Throwing a handful of sand into the air in a christening ritual and promulgating to the 40,000 that this was "to be called The Monocle, by jove," Carl acquired an idea he immediately passed on to the other co-president of the Beebuzzards: "Why not pretend to be two Oxford students over from England to do a bit of sociological research here in the States?"

"Simply pregnant, ol' cheroot, and quite bully and all that ol' stuff!" I approved. "But this singular impersonation might become tiresome in time. How about reserving it for some of the most visibly susceptible persons and assuming other roles to accommodate other personalities? And to a chosen few we might even be Carl Lewis and Lawrence Nelson."

My suggestions met with Sharkey's favor, and soon we were on our way to the administration building, brotherly love in our hearts and a hope to make our stay at Filmore one which the good brethren would remember with kindliness. As my buddy so aptly put it, "We might easily be Methodist ambassadors of good will here for the purpose of helping to bring the two denominations into greater mutual understanding and fellowship."

Although we were acquainted with no one here at the camp, we did know a name — A.B., Freeman. According to Cousin Julia, Freeman, a ranchman who had once aspired to be a minister but who later had become more interested in rounding up fat cattle than lost sheep, was one of the chief benefactors of this summer encampment.

After an inquiry, we found him at a table in the registration area.

Stout, red-faced, and fighting a losing battle against heat penetrating a galvanized roof, he gave us a sticky hand, a generous smile, and a pleasant greeting.

"You remember us from last year, of course," said Sharkey to the hairless man who had never before seen us.

And before his thick lips could wheeze an answer above his double chin, I said, "We're the Rice boys, Reverend Jasper O. Rice's sons. Surely you haven't forgotten us, Mr. Freeman!"

"Oh...er, why no, of course not. How're you boys?"

"Okay," I replied. "Dad sends his best regards, by the way, and the wish he could see you again. He always did get a big kick out of chewing the rag with you, Mr. Freeman."

"And there's nothing I enjoy more than a chat with him, boys. I'll declare you young men look more like your father every day."

We thanked him in unison, and I added, "You know how we feel about the Reverend, I guess. He's our ideal."

"And the ideal of some other folks, too," said the master of hypocrisy. "And how's the rest of the family?"

"Well, mom's been on the decline ever since our dear sis...Carl, you tell him about it. I'm afraid I'm just too emotional."

"You may have read about it in the papers, Mr. Freeman, although we appealed to the press, for mom's sake, to keep as much of it out as possible."

"Something about your sister, boys?" He invited us to sit down. My buddy took a chair opposite him, and I chose one immediately next to our host.

"I'm sure if dad were here, he'd tell you all about it," said Carl, "so I'm going to let you in on the entire tragedy. You see it started when poor sister came home early from work one afternoon and caught a professional fan dancer giving sister's unemployed husband a private demonstration."

"Was she pretty?" Mr. Freeman wanted to know. "And not quite so loud, young fella."

"Was she pretty! Why she was beauty personified. She used to be a physical training instructor at our college. You should have seen her stripped for gym!"

"Who was Jim?"

"I meant gymnasium, Mr. Freeman. She was a sun-tanned blonde with long, smooth legs. She was just a wee bit plump — ideally plump — a girl whose round contours...Mr. Freeman, maybe you'd rather not hear the rest of the story."

"Go on, young fella, but in a quieter voice, please! I'm listening with the utmost interest."

"But, Mr. Freeman, the lady who's been listening and waiting behind you, maybe to see you about something, is quite disgusted with this account."

"I most assuredly am, A.B. Freeman, and I don't see how you, a professed gentleman, can relish or even tolerate such vulgarity, particularly here on these grounds! I'm ashamed to say you were once a pupil of mine!"

"Now, Miss Peat," alibied the wrinkled maid's erstwhile pupil, his face red as a chigger bite, "I was just trying to get all the facts of a sad case."

"It certainly is a sad case. A.B."

"But these young men insisted on telling me about their family — a family that's very dear to me, Miss Peat."

"And, of course, you didn't ask them all about that...that hussy! And was it necessary for him to go into a detailed description of her...her physical being, A.B., and did you have to hang on every word as you did, A.B.?

"I'm afraid my first impression of you was a correct one. Ever since that recess when I caught you smoking fig leaves back of Mr. Goodwin's barn, I've been watching you, A.B., and wondering how you'd turn out. Well, I think I know the answer now."

Merciful at last, the disappointed schoolmistress pulled in her eyes, let her nostrils collapse to normality, and treaded away, leaving her human punching bag swathing his wet neck with a silken bandana.

"It's my fault, Mr. Freeman," confessed Carl, as he turned my way long enough to wink. "I shouldn't have talked so loud. But ever since mom became hard of hearing, I've become accustomed to talking loud."

"Mom wasn't deaf until all this trouble came up," I contributed. "The doctors say that her auditory nerves suffered a breakdown when Sissie...well, Carl can tell you about it."

"Yes? Well, go on with your story, young man — Carl, if you don't mind my calling you by your given name. I've heard your father speak of you so often, I feel I know you about as well as I know him."

"I really prefer it, sir, and I'm sure my brother would like for you to call him Lawrence."

"I surely would, Mr. Freeman. After all, you're somewhat like a relative, anyway. By the way, Carl, doesn't he remind you somehow of Uncle Filbert?"

"Well now, Carl and Lawrence, it makes me feel down-right good to hear you say that, and I feel honored that I remind you of your uncle. But about this trouble of your sister's and the, er...the entertainer you were about to tell me about when that old fos...I mean Miss Peat butted in. I declare I'd like to have a dime for every time she's scolded me."

"Well, when this beautiful fan dancer...Mr. Freeman, you ought to see her. She's giving shows, by the way, now not too far from here at...but that's all beside the point."

"Well, now, young fella, I think in a case like this we ought to know all the facts. Where's she working?"

Sharkey named a nearby town, a fictitious night club, and continued his narrative.

"Well, when sis came in and saw this beautiful blonde branishing her unveiled charms for the benefit of Peter — that's her hubby — the blonde ran for cover and sis ran for Peter with her little .32 automatic she used to carry in her purse when she dated him before their marriage. Unfortunately, Peter didn't have on his shoes and when he started out across the vacant lot behind the house the stickers slowed him down and...well, the judge said he was lenient when he gave her ten years."

"It's a sad case," sympathized Miss Peat's ex-problem pupil. "And your mother?"

"We had to confine her to an institution soon after the trial. And then there's Jasper Jr., or Bud, as we sometimes call him."

"Yes?"

"Jasper Jr., I'm sure you've heard dad say, is our older brother who dropped out of school to help dad send us to college."

"Oh, yes, I think I remember now."

"He's our immediate concern right now," I put in, after Carl had given me one of his you-get-in-on-this-deal-too looks. "You see, not long after sis went to the penitentiary, Bud's boss made a comment about her and then Carl and I caught him on a dark street one night. When the man came back from the hospital a week later, he fired our brother. We seem to be a marked family, Mr. Freeman. People say we're too hot-tempered. They even say it about dad, and just because he knocked the postman down the steps for saying mom was peculiar.

And, by the way, he's thinking about resigning and becoming an undertaker. He said it would be a pleasure to deal, for a change, with people who don't talk."

"Dad's a great man, Mr. Freeman," Sharkey cut in to say.

"Of course he is," agreed the human sweatbox.

"But back to Jasper," I resumed. "He can't get a job. People are afraid of our tempers. But Bud doesn't have any temper at all, Mr. Freeman. I remember a few years ago Carl and I, by way of experiment, tried to find it with a rubber hose. We'd been whaling our brother for about twenty minutes when a neighbor stopped us by threatening to call the police, so we didn't have an opportunity to obtain a really scientific conclusion. We meant to try it again before Bud recuperated from his attack of pneumonia, but somehow we never got around to it."

"What did your dad say about your abusing your brother?"

"Oh," I said, "he's a good sport, you know. He just laughed and said a little chastisement sometimes was good for everybody."

"Dad's a great fellow," repeated Sharkey.

"It just occurred to me, Mr. Freeman," said I, "that you are a ranchman and that Bud is a ranchman. You have a big ranch and Bud doesn't have a job."

"I see what you mean, young fella, and I think maybe I can use him. Get him over to my Bar C Ranch on Thursday of next week and we'll put him to work right away."

"Dad always said you were a great scout" was my grateful assurance. "But I wonder if you would let Bud wait two weeks before reporting for work? His new artificial leg ought to be in by then, and moreover, we need some time in which to get him fitted up with another pair of glasses. We're hoping that a new pair of specs will enable him to recognize a cow at 70 yards at least."

"You mean he's got a wooden leg and he can't recognize a cow at 70 yards! And you want me to give him a job as a cowboy? Why...why, half the herd would be beyond his vision half the time. Why, we'd have strays all over the state!"

"But, Mr. Freeman, it's his uncanny sense of hearing he relies on," I explained. "Dr. Hogue said that that cow's kicking him in the head may have affected him otherwise but it certainly didn't harm his sense of hearing. In fact, the doctor says Bud's hearing capacity seems even greater because of the hoofing. Surely, Mr. Freeman, you're not going to tear down our dreams for a happy family just because of a few little irrelevant details! Bud can't help having that strawberry complexion and a bay window. You are going to give him this chance for happiness, aren't you, Mr. Freeman?"

The rancher was about to answer when a bold clanging from the mess hall claimed his attention.

"There it is," said he, "the come-and-get-it signal. Now if you young fellas will come along with me, I'd like to introduce you as my special guests for this meal."

"And by the way," he added just as Sharkey and I were about to exchange victory glances, "if I'm to introduce you to some of my friends, I'd sure like to have your real names."

It was a good story, he told us with a laugh, and we were "quite imaginative but we were not deceptive," and he doubted that we had the acting ability we needed in order to successfully assume identities other than our own.

Would he care to make a wager?

His position among his fellows and his religious scruples, he said, would not permit him to bet. Then would he make an agreement? In the event we succeeded in convincing at least two persons of 16 years of age or older that we were visiting students from England, would he be willing to come to breakfast clad only in his pajamas?

"Yes," he replied after a moment of deliberation "provided you work under a time limit of two hours from the time you finish your lunch. And, of course, if you fail in your impersonation, you'll be the ones who'll answer the bell in pajamas. Okay?"

"Okay," without its question mark, bounced back at him like twin echoes.

But for our recent defeat and this agreement, the midday meal of long pintos, syrupy prunes, and barbecued beef would have seemed more enjoyable to us "Rice boys."

Without partaking of our habitual second helping, we thanked our host for his hospitality, we reminded him to prepare his night clothes for promenading in public, and then we sought the privacy of The Monocle — there to rest and plan our latest project.

CHAPTER TWENTY-TWO

Duel in the Pasture

Comfortable on cots under a sheltering mountain oak, we were working at final details when a pretty high school brunette treaded timidly upon us and apologized with: "I'm sorry to have to come around and disturb you at this time of day, but it's about the only time we can find everybody at home, and we've got to get our census finished by tomorrow."

"It's all right," said I, before woman-hating Sharkey could put in his "have a seat on that luxurious boulder behind you."

"Thanks," she responded, her chestnut eyes spotlighting her apparent naiveness, "but I'm afraid I'll soil my dress."

"Bravo for chivalry, the gem of the South!" exclaimed my chum when I covered the rough rock with one of his new shirts.

"Thank you, sir," said the young Baptist, sitting down on the padded boulder.

"And now, young lady," said I, "be assured that we are yours, body and soul, but for the asking. Meanwhile, be assured that we stand up tiptoe, ready to serve you in whatever capacity we can."

"Well, we have to get everybody's name and where they're from, so I want to get yours."

"And I guess you want our phone numbers, too," said Lewis. "Shame on you running around a Christian encampment and asking strange men their names and telephone numbers. Suppose your mother found out about your conduct? Now wouldn't you...."

"But I didn't ask you for your telephone number."

"Then I feel slighted," I hurried to say.

"But I didn't ask anybody's number."

"A likely story, a likely story."

"But I didn't."

"But, but, but! Haven't your English teachers told you to avoid buts at the beginning of sentences?"

"Yes, but...."

"There you go again. Seems to me you've gotten yourself in a but rut. You ought to increase your word power so that you won't have to depend on a but to get you a date."

"But I'm not trying to get a date!" she flared almost delicately.

"Don't look now, but you just stubbed your tooth on another but."

"Come on now, Carl," I appealed, "the lady's here on business. Let's cooperate."

"I'll be dern if she'll make a customer out of me! I didn't help pull that last bank job and risk playing host to a necktie party just to throw it away on a skirt, Slug...I mean Lawrence."

"Be careful, Spider, or you'll have the young lady thinking we're a pair of desperados."

By now her expression of resentment had surrendered to fear. She was going to have to hurry along, she told us.

"Oh, yeah? challenged Carl, adopting a rougher tone and diction. "Well, not before you get our names and addresses! Just because we pulled a coupla...I mean just because we carry a coupla .45 Colts is no reason why you should omit our names from the register."

"Well, we do want to get everybody's name and address, all right."

"Okay then, Lawrence, give her the names of everyone in our gang — yeah, everyone who shares this tent with us."

The girl looked questioningly at the two-man pup tent but said nothing.

"Well, in the first place, all of us live in Beebuzzard, Texas. The members of our group are Carl Lewis, Sharkey Lewis...."

"We're not supposed to get any nicknames, please."

"Oh, so you don't want any nicknames!" sneered Sharkey. "Now listen, sis, you take what we dish out and like it, see? Now if we knew Sharkey's first name, we'd let you have it, but we don't. The same goes for Lefty Nelson, Lawrence's bud. When a guy joins our gang we accept the names they give us and ask no questions."

If it occurred to the high schooler to wonder why I would not know my own brother's given name, she did not express her wonder. Instead she asked, "Is that all of the people that stay with you?"

When we had supplied her with four more names, we invited her to come back to see "the boys," and then I relieved her confusion by wishing her a good afternoon.

Shoes shining and ties waving, we proceeded soon afterwards to the recreation grounds. There we met a pair of late teenage welterweights who called themselves CX and Glenn.

In an overdone British accent and in a manner dripping with effeminacy, Carl interrupted their Ping-Pong singles with: "I say, ol' chaps, my brotha and I should jolly well like to oppose you in a game of this — what do you American fellows call it?"

They gasped, looked at one another, and laughed.

CX then ran a hand through his sandy hair, drew his freckled face taut, and drawled, "Why you wanta talk like that?"

"I beg your pawdon, ol' boy, but I'm afraid I don't know what you mean."

"Whatta you wanta give us that ol' ah-stuff for and talk like a sissy?"

"But, my good fellow, I'm simply speaking the King's English as I have always bean taught to speak it. I'm dreadfully sorry that you resent it."

"Aw, it's okay, I guess. I jest don't like it."

"Me neither," spoke up swarthy Glen, rolling a sleeve higher to give more display to a set of knobby biceps. "Where you guys from, anyway?"

"My deah American youth," said I, joining in the British tone, "we hail from Gloucester, England, home of the immortal William Ernest Henley, whose famed 'Invictus' has given us our philosophy and our way of life. Perhaps you recall the first stanza of his great work:

> " `Out of the night that covers me,
>   Black as the Pit from pole to pole,
> I thank whatever gods may be
>   For my unconquerable soul.' "

"Would you like to hear another inspiring stanza?"

To Glen's answer of "Heck no!" I responded, "You're not being true to yourself, ol' cheroot. Eyes are the windows of the soul, and I can see in your delightfully green eyes that you are in reality a genuine lover of the fine arts. But you refuse to admit this truth, even to yourself."

"Sir Leftylot," said Sharkey, "how well the renowned Chaucer describes this unfortunate fellow's case when he says:

> " `Whan that Aprille with his shoures sote
> The droghte of Marche hath perced to the rote,
> And bathed every veyne in....' "

"Do you know what the heck you're sayin'?" butted in CX.

"Naw, they're jest trying' to show off," theorized his companion.

"Yeah, an' they're nuts, too, jest like all them English foreigners."

"Sir," said I, "were we on the campus at Oxford, our associates would jolly well take you to task for your disparaging remarks."

"Indeed they would! They'd give you the tongue-lashing of your life."

To this CX sneered, "Yeah, but I doubt if they'd have the guts to put up their dukes."

"Oh yes, they would" was the other Beebuzzard's assurance, "and they'd put up their earls and counts as well as their dukes."

"That ain't what I mean. I mean, would they fight?"

"You mean resort to fisticuffs — come to blows?"

"Yeah."

"But gentlemen don't engage in common brawls, my inimical ignoramus."

"Whatta'd you call me?" His arms cocked at 90-degree angles, CX bristled into breathing distance of my "Oxford" classmate.

"Why, ol' fellow, I simply called you an ignoramus...nothing to be offended about, don't you know?"

"Well, that's all right. But I thought you called me something else."

"Not at all, my good friend. I don't wish to be offensive, even when I say that your reeking breath is quite contaminating, in fact beastly obnoxious."

"Whatta'd you say about my breath?" Again the freckled one advanced closer.

"I simply said that your breath...I say, ol' man, you really ought to do something about that halitosis of yours. Do you know that, according to statistics, 90 per...."

"Yeah, well listen you, how'd you like for me to fix you up like George Washington done them other English guys?"

At this point I came in with: "I say now, the fellow's better educated than I thought. Why, he's actually heard about the first president of his country."

"You stay out of this, see?" It was Glenn's turn to come forward and assume the 90-degree arm angle.

"Glenn," said CX, "you set that sissy guy on his twatt, and I'll set this un on his."

"Please, gentleman, not here — please," I entreated. "Please set us on our twatts in a more private place."

"Okay then," granted CX. "Where you wanta go to get what's comin' to you?"

We led the way toward a small valley that lay just beyond the rocky rim of our camping area.

At our tent we stopped and my buddy and I proposed that we borrow a set of "boxing mittens" from two of our friends, Lefty and Sharkey, who "on occasions had used the things to strike one another ever so hard."

When Sharkey and Lefty failed to answer our calls, I walked to The Carcass and "borrowed" the gloves.

Having reached our destination, Glenn began lacing on his friend's gloves, while I laced Sharkey's.

"Goodness," said I, "this is almost like a duel scene one sees at the cinema! Are you nervous, my deah Carl?"

"Quite so, brotha."

"You sure would be nervous," Glenn assured, "if you could see how CX knocked out a guy at the Sportatorium one night. Me and CX have both fought there. Bet you guys ain't even had a glove on before."

Why tell these pugnacious lads that during the last three years or more we had worn out two sets of gloves, that boxing was our sports hobby, and that we kept in fighting shape the year round? They probably wouldn't have believed us any more than they believed Lewis when he said, "Oh, but we have had on the mittens before, my ingenuous proletarian. We received training from an instructor at Oxford who tutored us for two whole weeks in the art of self defense. I do hope I can recall the instructions he gave me."

"You're a dern liar" was CX's accusation. "You ain't ever put the gloves on. I can tell that by the way you're looking at them dern gloves."

"Oh, but you're mistaken, my deah fellow. And why must you use that beastly word you just used? Really, I find it quite difficult to understand why chaps of your type should be attracted to an encampment like these good people are holding."

The matter was none of our business, CX assured, us, but he would tell us anyway. They had followed "a coupla women to the place and when we get 'em where we want 'em we sure ain't gonna be readin' the Bible with 'em."

"In that case, BX, I shall be compelled to deal with you rather roughly."

"CX is my name, you!"

"All right then, my deah GX."

"Sure wish some of the gang was here, Glenn. They'd sure get a kick outa what I'm gonna do to this guy."

Fully laced now, the duelists stood facing one another in a clearing, a sort of rustic arena of nature's creation — a ring, the ropes of which were encircling rocks and the canvas of which was stock-leveled grass.

"On guard, sir," Carl warned, purposely assuming an awkward stance.

"Look at 'im standin' there, Glenn," smirked CX. "He's got a guard like a washwoman!"

"Swat 'im flat with the ol' one-two, CX!" urged Glenn.

"It ain't gonna take two. I'm jest gonna give 'im the ol' CX Special and watch 'im take a dive."

His words echoing among the boulders, the overconfident boxer charged his opponent, and, without bothering to feint, unleased a vicious right that glanced wildly off the back of Sharkey's sparrying left.

The instant CX's blow spent its force, Sharkey hit his adversary with a neat right cross that landed against the latter's ear to register an expression which seemed to reveal pain and then dismay.

Withdrawing from the close-ups exchange, CX began to circle the now graceful and nimble Sharkey, who had abandoned his pretense at inexperience in boxing and was now giving the Sportatorium fighter a lesson in footwork.

Having recovered from the effects of the right cross, CX came in again, feinted with both fists, drove an ineffective right into Sharkey's middle, received a jarring face lifting, and backed out. But this time Sharkey followed, covering him with punishing blows and combinations.

And then suddenly it was all over. In an effort to shield his ear from another attack, the self-avowed girl chaser had left his jaw unguarded for an instant. During that instant he who allegedly had received training from an instructor at Oxford laid heavy leather on his opponent and brought him floundering earthward.

"I say, ol' boy," said the perpendicular victor to the horizontal vanquished, "I'm frightfully sorry. I trust you didn't alight on any stones, PX."

"I ain't ever been did this way before," moaned groggy CX through a mouth of bubbling crimson.

"You really pack a wallop," said Glenn to Sharkey when we had fanned CX to a sitting position. "I guess you can lick your brother with one hand, can't you?"

"Well, hardly, my deah fellow. In fact, fawther says we're the most evenly matched strikers he's ever known. By the way, didn't your partner say something about your setting him on his twatt, as you call it?"

Glenn's mouth seemed to sag a bit, his arms fell out of their swaggering angles, and somehow his sleeves seemed to droop a trifle.

"Who? Me fight your brother? Shoot, me an' him are good friends.

CHAPTER TWENTY-THREE

Strip Tease in the Doctor's Office

Time romped along with us into mid-September — immediate prologue to pacific autumn, when the frolicking Mesa wind, weary of sandpapering the valley, becomes less active...when the sunflowers, having nodded greetings throughout the summer, also acknowledge their bygone prime and bemoan with drooping heads their wanning beauty...when the apple and pear trees, long having fought predatory gusts to retain their young fruit, sense the nearness of weaning time and kiss their offspring with dewy lips and then let them fall to freedom on the earth.

After we had enrolled this morning at the college for the fall semester, Carl and I came back to my house for dinner. Having enjoyed a delightful gorging on enchiladas and hominy, we made our sluggish way into the living room and slouched into the couch.

"You know, guy, I think we're reforming to some extent," my stuffed guest managed to say as he sucked on a mangled toothpick.

"And your evidence?"

"Well, we've about ceased victimizing people indiscriminately. In fact, we haven't molested anyone unless he molested us first since we jumped the little census taker."

"Oh, but what about our placing the can of burning rags in Mr. Freeman's cabin the night he said he wasn't going through with the pajama deal?"

"That man must have half suffocated before he woke up," chuckled Carl.

"And half awake at that, else he wouldn't have come running out and yelling something about a branding iron."

"We really got the ol' boy out in his pajamas all right, didn't we though? Too bad he didn't have a bigger audience. A show like that deserved more than a mere 25 or 30 people."

Waiting for her mother to bathe her and send her to her room for a nap, my little sister wandered in, took a seat between us, and handed me a big orange.

"Bubber," said the 4-year-old, "skin me this like you skin some rabbits."

"I have to wait on you too much, young lady. Now why don't you do it?"

"I can't, bubber, I don't got much hands."

"I think I'll start calling you `Can't'."

I had undressed the orange, halved it, and was handing it to Helen when she said, "Make it littler, bubber, 'cause I don't have much mouth."

"Yum, yum," she exclaimed upon tasting the juicy fruit, "this better than that corn on the stob mama fix me for supper two yesterdays!"

Next she turned to my chum with: "Why you don't go outside and swing me up real high and let me rain down?"

"Honey, I'm too full to do much moving around. Suppose I just tell you a story instead?"

"Okay. What you gonna tell me 'bout?"

"Well, now let's see. Suppose I tell you 'bout a horse?"

"Okay."

"Well, once upon a time there was a horse that lived on top of a hill. One day he became thirsty and went...."

"Why he didn't drink some milk an' get him a big stomach like Cousin Julia?"

"But this animal didn't drink milk; it made him belch. And nice horses don't like to do that."

"They jest like nice childrens. Huh? Tell me some more 'bout the horse."

"Well, the horse looked all around him for some water. Finally he saw a deep pond in the valley below. `Now,' said he to himself, `if it would just rain, it would fill up the pond and I'd have some water to drink and...' "

"If I was that horse I'd jest tell Jesus an' He'd throw down some water an' I'd open my mouth an' get watered all I wanted. What else did the horse do?"

"Finally it did rain and when the horse saw the pond was full, he started running down to the valley. But before he reached the pond, a chicken drank up all the water."

"You know what, Carl? That horse jest like Cousin Boyd. Mama say he drinks all the time. What else the horse do? Huh?"

" `Why didn't you save some for me?' said the horse to the chicken. And the chicken replied, `There was just enough for me.' So the horse went back to the top of the hill and waited for more rain."

"Then what?"

Rain fell again, once more the parched quadruped descended to the pond only to find that the imbibing hen had repeated her self-saturation, and again she explained, 'There was just enough for me.'

Unable to beat the chicken to the pond in the valley, the patient horse was making a fourth trip to his watchtower on the horizon when my mother stopped the story with: "Helen, it's time for your bath."

"But Carl got to finish 'bout the horse!" sobbed the disappointed child. "He don't have any water! He's gonna die an' get all white an' get throwed in a hole!"

Upon learning the rest of the story, her parent made a partially spelled-out appeal to the narrator: "Please, for goodness sakes, l-e-t the animal g-e-t some w-a-t-e-r this time!"

And so just as the hen began to drink again "she exploded like a balloon" and the horse drank and drank until the water ran out of his mouth, and then and then only did the dove of peace come to roost again in the Nelson household.

Helen had just pattered away to her bed and my mother had just reminded my father to "stop shoveling in the cow barn and come rest awhile," when Sharkey proposed that we "rattle down to Doc Hogue's office and get our R.O.T.C. physicals."

At the corner of Main and Cypress we picked up another student whose name we knew had automatically slated him, too, for this afternoon's examination of all Yucca males in the G to O bracket. He was Harry McDonald, a lanky toe-headed freshman whose features and manners were ever ready to declare him a true son of the soil.

"I sure hope I pass this exam," he said, "because someday I'm gonna join the army and be a captain. That's my ambition. That's the only reason I'm goin' to college. Paw wants me to specialize in ag and help him with the dairy, but I aim to be an army man."

"Major Hoople," as we had titled the boy because of his tendency to be talkative and boastful like the noted comic character, doubled up his fist to show us his muscle.

"Look at that!" he ejaculated without trying to conceal his pride. "I sure don't see how they can turn me down when they get a look at that bulge. Boy, I can push a heifer over with that...and I'm only seventeen at that. And you oughta see how many times I can chin myself. Guess how many."

The Major was chagrined at our guesses of six and seven. Twenty-two was his speed, he told us.

He wondered "what all they'll exam us for."

"Oh, Dr. Hogue will give you a series of eye and ear tests, a check-up with his stethoscope, and then run a couple of laboratory tests," enlightened Sharkey.

"Ever have a blood test made, Harry?" I inquired.

"No, I never did. How they do it?"

Now was my chance, I thought, to revenge the not unrequited advances Harry had made toward Alice during the past three vacation months. And why had she been attracted to him? She had merely been amused by the novelty of his unshod mannerisms, I like to assure myself.

"They're not very pleasant," I told him.

"Why? What do they do?"

"Oh, doc will just run a long needle in your leg and drain off about a pint of blood for some mic tests."

"How long's the needle?"

"About three inches, I guess. No doubt you've seen the long swordlike type of needle your dad or the veterinarian uses in vaccinating your dad's cows. A blood test needle will look just about like it."

"Well, gosh, he won't stick it all the way in, will he?"

"Why, certainly. Why do you suppose he uses a needle that long, if he isn't going to shove it all the way in?"

"You bet he shoves it all in — right up to the very hilt," cooperated Lewis.

"But I always thought the doctor just stuck the needle in a vein."

"So he does," said I, "but the vein Dr. Hogue goes after is situated next to the bone in the fatty portion of the leg, halfway between the knee and the hip."

Arriving at the office of our examining physician, we were happy to observe that, save an old lady, the place was without patients. I had been afraid that the office would be crowded with examinees and that the freshman would obtain a more truthful description of a blood test. Evidently, we were early arrivals.

The doctor, busy at the moment, would see us shortly, said his receptionist, after she had checked our names on a list supplied by the college Military Department.

We had been seated about five minutes when the patient within screamed in pain.

"Wonder what th' heck he's doin' to her?" said Major Hoople.

"He could be giving her a blood test" was my suggestion.

"Well, gosh, does it hurt that much?"

"Sometimes. He may have struck the bone in this poor woman."

While my associate was explaining to our listener why doctors did not administer anesthesia when making these tests, I walked to the farther end of the room and asked the office miss for the time.

Another scream later, I returned to the concerned freshman to falsify, "Yep, I was right. The girl at the counter said that the patient just got a blood test."

Another cry of pain.

"Well, what's she still hollerin' 'bout?" Harry wanted to know. "It don't hurt that long, does it?"

"Well, it seems that the doctor broke off about two inches of needle in her leg, and now he's trying to cut it out."

"Good gosh, I sure hope that don't happen to me. Say, can't we possibly make the R.O.T.C. without gettin' a blood test? I don't have any disease. My folks can give Major Walters a statement sayin' I haven't. He oughta know — my own paw!"

"Easy now, Harry," consoled Sharkey. "Chances are you may not suffer all the agony that poor, unfortunate soul is experiencing."

Another scream gave the Major's face an additional whitewashing, pushed him down farther in his chair, and divested him of further inclination to talk.

Suddenly a door snapped open and tall, heavy, unconventional Dr. Alvin Hogue, his red head surrounded by cigar smoke and bumping up and down in time with his long swinging arms, approached Sharkey and me and beckoned us forward out of hearing range of Harry and the elderly lady.

Son of the man who had first spanked breath into me some 19 years backward, Dr. "Alvin," as we in the family were accustomed to call him, was glad to see me "and that perpetual sidekick of yours."

"Boys," he said, "you're just the pair I'm looking for. Knowing you as I do, I think myself safe in saying you're just made to order for this particular job...if you'll do it for me."

"Just name it, Doctor Alvin," said I.

"Well, I've got a young woman inside who's been coming to me for skin treatments for three months now without paying me so much as a dime. Now gentleman, I'm sympathetic to the ills and sufferings that befall mortal man, but, by golly, I'm a human being myself and I've got to eat, too.

"Now I do treat several charity cases each month, but, by golly, this is not one of them. If this young woman can't pay her own bill, she ought to get that money-cloaked dad of hers to slip me the dough. Any guy that can provide his son and daughter each with a big car a block long can sure pay his daughter's bills. But, by golly, he won't. So from this day forward, she'll go to somebody else. I've told her before I don't want to treat her any longer, but she keeps coming back and telling me, 'Doctor, you *are* going to treat me, do you understand?'

"Maybe you heard her yellin'? I've been giving her subcutaneous shots. I could have made them intramuscular or intravenous, but I wanted to be sure they hurt. Soon as I got the needle under her skin, I wormed it up and down a few times. Gentlemen, it's not that I'm sadistic, it's just that I don't want a wealthy patient who won't pay me what's coming to me!"

We didn't blame him a bit, we assured him.

"Now then, gentlemen, I can't help but remember that I'm a doctor and that as such should not inflict unnecessary physical pain, so I'm not going to jab her further, but, by golly, I'm going to make sure she doesn't take up any more of my time.

"Now then, I just told the young woman to strip down to bear necessities and crawl up on the X-ray table. If you're game, just come on in with me and we'll see that she doesn't come back."

"Right this way, gentlemen!" the man of medicine half shouted for the benefit of his unwelcome patient, who, tummy-up and clawing madly for cover, reddened with embarrassment and turned her face to the wall...but not before we had recognized her.

"Miss Snerd," said the doctor, "I just wanted these young men to see the nature of your skin disease before we give you any more treatments. Now when you come back next time, I want them to be here again so they can observe whether or not we're making any progress. You see, I'm liable to look at those ugly pimples on your back and just imagine they're drying up, because I might be prejudiced. But Mr. Nelson and Mr. Lewis here, being disinterested parties, won't be. Now then, gentlemen, if you'll just move in closer, please."

"Dr. Hogue, is this really necessary?" said Bossy Betsy.

"Of course it is, Miss Snerd."

"Well, I wish you hadn't selected those two. You don't know them like I do."

"Oh, but I do know them...very well, my dear. Now then if you'll please stop trying to conceal yourself, we'd like to look you over a little more closely."

"You needn't be so touchy, Betsy," said Sharkey, "we're not seeing anything we didn't see the night you participated in the bathing beauty show."

"I don't want to talk to you, Mr. Lewis!" returned the bare one.

"Doctor," said I, alluding to her slightly misshapen legs, "what causes bowleggedness."

"Lawrence Nelson, I'll have you know I'm not bowlegged. I'm...well, you should have heard the compliment Professor Holdbolt paid my figure."

"Oh ho!" ejaculated Sharkey. "The boss has been noticing your form, huh? Tell me, Miss Snerd, have you gotten a raise recently?"

"Oh you...you, oh, but I hope you take something under Professor Holdbolt this year and I get to grade your papers, Carl Lewis. Maybe you think I won't grade them right down to the last comma!"

"Dr. Alvin," said I, "there's another lad in the outer office it might be well to have in on this scrutinizing. His dad has a dairy and he knows a lot about cows."

"Why, sure, Lawrence, get him in here," instructed the unpaid physician. "The more the merrier."

"Get that ol' lady, too, Lefty!" Carl called after me.

Closing the door behind me, I walked across the outer office floor to Freshman McDonald.

"You get your test?" he inquired weakly.

"Nope. The doctor just had us holding down his patient while he gouged around for that needle."

"He get through?"

"Finally. She helped us by passing out cold."

"Harry," I told him after a pause, "Dr. Hogue wants you to come on in. He's going to line us up and sock it to us."

"Can't I wait a little bit, Lawrence. I'm kinda sick at the stomach. Dad told me I hadn't ort to eat all four of those pork chops for dinner."

"Come on, Harry, the doctor's waiting. He's got the needles sterilized and he's all ready to slam them in."

I took him by the arm, he rose reluctantly, and we started across the floor.

Suddenly Harry threw his weight against me, and sank to the floor.

Before the office girl could summon her employer, I soaked my handkerchief in water from the nearby fountain and slapped it repeatedly across the freshman's face.

He opened his eyes just as Dr. Hogue bent over to feel his pulse.

"No, doctor!" he pleaded half consciously, "No, no, not today! I ate too much pork. I don't want that rammin' today, I tell you! I'm not even gonna be in the R.O.T.C...might not even go to college. I'm sick, I tell you!"

High heels clicked by, leaving a brief breath of perfume.

"Good afternoon, Miss Snerd," said the doctor to departing Bossy Betsy.

The sole sound now was a series of groans from Harry.

CHAPTER TWENTY-FOUR

Joshing the Book Agent

Stripped to the waist and sticky with perspiration and apple juice, Sharkey released his end of a cider press handle and gave audience to 10-year-old Enrique, our harvest "foreman" whose crew of boys had this Saturday gathered about 26 bushels of worm-grounded fruit for us from Mr. Lewis' orchard of some 96 trees.

"The fellows are all through, Carl," the swarthy little Latin American reported without noticeable accent. "I made them do just as you said do — put the extry wormy ones in one pile and the not-so-rotten wormy ones in another."

"Good work, Enrique," complimented Sharkey.

"Now you ready for me to start the fight?"

"No, Enrique, there won't be any fight this year."

"No fight this year! You mean you not gonna let me start a fight so you can run the gang all off like you do every year so you won't have to pay them for workin' today?"

"No, we're actually going to pay each and every lad this year...but it's going to have to be in pay cider."

"Pay cider," as we called it, was our more inferior brand of cider which we pressed from the poorer quality apples. This was the cider we used in paying Enrique. But Enrique didn't mind. He simply added an additional injection of sodium benzoate to give the beverage pungency and sold it to his neighbors...at least his original customers were his neighbors. Later he learned to avoid trying to sell his product to previous purchasers. It must have been the artificial cake coloring he used in enhancing the salability of the juice, we told Enrique, that was responsible for the dissatisfaction which not infrequently accompanied his sales. Surely the beverage as it left us was free of injurious ingredients, for we were ever careful to remove all bits of uncrushed worms from our produce, and, moreover, we strained it.

"Well, gee whiz, Carl," argued our employee, "I don't see why you wanta pay these kids. They won't do nothing but buy cigarettes with the money they get from selling their cider, anyway. Besides, they're liable to sell to some people I got picked out for customers. Come on, Lawrence, you get Carl to let me pick the fight like we always do. Come on, Carl, grab you up some clods and some green apples and get ready to do some bustin'!"

"Now, listen, Enrique, Lawrence and I have talked this matter over thoroughly and we've decided and we're resolved to give the boys a fair deal this season, so call 'em up and pour out a quart of pay cider for each one. You can use some of those cans and jars under the hay barn for containers."

"Okay, you're the bosses. But there's one good thing in it for me: I won't haft to go to a lotta trouble rounding up a new bunch of workers next year like I always had to do. Maybe I can get these same kids back."

He was about to call them in to meet the pay roll when another idea struck him: "Why don't we jest make each kid drink their quart now and we won't haft to clean up all those jars and cans?"

"Enrique," said I, "you're still afraid your buddies are going to beat you to your customers, aren't you?"

Half an hour later, as we watched brown heads bobbing and legs swinging away on Enrique's burro-drawn wagon, Sharkey remarked, "I'll bet that scheming little rascal will get some of their cider for taking them to town."

Having cleaned our press and barreled the fruits of our labors, we sparred a couple of rounds with the gloves and then struck out on a mile of roadwork through the orchard and into a cotton field toward the irrigation canal.

Above us was a blue Western sky. Distantly ahead, the spires and knolls of a purple mountain. Immediately ahead, the knobs of white on stalks of brown. Behind and around us, the fragrance of ripe apples blending with the sweetness of alfalfa and the freshness of adobe dankness.

Youthfully primed to enjoy the earth and sky, we raced along together, eyeing and smelling and listening, tingling with health and vigor.

At the edge of the canal, we slipped off our clothing. The white foam and adobe-loaded water, looking like frosty meringue upon a chocolate pudding, parted to admit us into a current that immediately challenged us to pit our strength against its own and swim to the water gate a duck quack northward.

Panting but victorious, we had crawled out on the bank when Carl noted that a car had turned into the Lewis driveway.

"I doubt that the folks have come back yet," said he, "so maybe we'd better run in and see who it is."

Just as we reached the back door, we glimpsed a spectacled, middle-aged lady nursing a satchel next to her bosom and approaching the front entrance.

"Book saleswoman, sure as I'm a Lewis. And if it is, watch me do some real joshing."

Bare-footed and shirtless, Sharkey responded to the visitor's knock with a "Howdy, ma'am."

I watched from the bathroom.

"Good afternoon," she returned.

"What's good about it, ma'am? We's lost two herd o' sheep, one of the hogs got himself made bacon of trying' to out-rassle a barbed wire fence, and my dog's done took sick. Hope you'll 'scuse me goin' 'round almost naked like this. I ain't had no shirt to wear since maw started takin' in washin'. Times shore is hard, ain't they, though? Reckon we'll jest haft to pull in our belts, though, and suck on our teeth. Sure feel sorry for you, though. You ain't got no belt to pull in, have you? Reckon you look like you got a corset though. What kin I do for you, ma'am?"

"Well, I...this is the Lewis residence, isn't it?" Her gray eyebrows stood up on stilts and her delicate lips puckered nervously.

"Reckon nobody better not say it ain't the Lewis dump, if they wanta eat vitals again. If you ever hear somebody say this ain't, ma'am, you jest let me know an' see if I don't snatch somebody up by his big toe and wrap his backbone 'round the first telephone pole that's handy. What do you want, ma'am? Git the lead out and speak up! You sellin' books?"

"Why...why, yes, as a matter of fact...yes, I am."

"Well, now, ma'am, that ain't nothin' to brag about. Shoot, I had an uncle onct that had a whole bushel o' books to sell, and he didn't go 'round spoutin' off at the mouth and braggin' 'bout it."

"Well, I'm not bra...."

"Now, ma'am, didn't nobody ever tell you it ain't perlite to go interruptin'? Shucks, we got a pair of ol' sows that won't even do that. If one of 'em starts scratchin' her bohunkas on a rail, the other jest waits 'til she gits through 'fore she scratches hern. You got pitchers in them books?"

"Yes," said the lady, backing away, apparently intent on departing. Why try to sell books to a rustic imbecile who quite obviously wouldn't even be capable of reading their titles?

"Now wait a minute, ma'am. Don't do nothin' hasty and rush off. Lemme call my uncle. I heard him talkin' 'bout buyin' a book one time. Oh, Uncle Lawrence!"

"Comin', nephew," I responded.

"Uncle Lawrence, this here's a woman that wants to sell you some books."

"Lady," said I, likewise bare to the waist, "you ain't got no second-handed shirt to sell, have you? We wanta go in to town tonight and do a little sparkin' but we ain't got no shirts, 'cept dirty ones that smell like they was drug through a skunk farm."

"Now don't go worryin' 'bout that, Uncle Lawrence. We kin always wear our raincoats an' them gals ain't gonna ever know we ain't got nothin' underneath."

"Lady, yore books got any pitchers o' purty gals in 'em like them that comes on calendars 'round Christmas time?"

"Why...no, the books I have to offer are entirely educational."

"Lady," I said, "if you knowed gals like I do, you'd know there ain't nothin' more educational."

"Wal," I appended, after a pause, "reckon then, we can't make no deal, if yore books ain't got no pitchers wurth lookin' at. We ain't got no money, nohow...couldn't buy a lick off a sodee pop bottle. But we're shore gonna slick up with olive oil and talcum powder and make them gals think our pockets is rippin' with coin, ain't we, nephew?"

"Yeah, we shore are, uncle. They ain't nothin' to look at. In fact, one look at them silly gals would turn a sow's belly, but that don't make no difference, 'cause their paw's got a piece o' ground an' a little bungalow and we could move in with their folks come hitchin' day. Course with a family o' eight souls... hey, wait a minute, ma'am, you ain't heard all the story. Ain'tcha got no romance in yore bones?"

"Yeah, stick around fer a spell, lady. We might let you be best man an' you'd git to kiss the brides fer us, 'cause we shore don't wanta."

CHAPTER TWENTY-FIVE

Mixing It at the Mixer

Old Sol, like a bloodshot eye weary from playing too much Peeping Tom, was descending in red on the western horizon when The Carcass stopped before the Goodman home and we alighted with five gallons of our deluxe sweet cider for our Epworth League's high school and college mixer, an occasion enjoyed each year on the parsonage lawn.

"How're you fellers?" inquired Foxy Mack from a ladder on the lawn. He was stringing a line of electric lights from one cottonwood to another.

"Okay, Mr. McSkinny."

"Fine, Mr. McPenny. Has anyone else arrived?"

"Nope, jist you fellers. The preacher and Mrs. Goodman've done gone to town after some cream and stuff, but the ol' lady's in there, I think."

"We'll take our cider in, and then we'll come back and help you finish your job, Mr. McSkinny," I promised him.

"That'll be dandy. I always did know I could count on you fellers."

To bring Mother Goodman to the latched screen, Carl punched the doorbell, I boxed the wall with a fist and we both gave our vocal cords a workout.

"I thought maybe I heard someone at the door," she said, at last coming into view. "But I wasn't sure."

It was Sharkey's turn to yell our introduction this time: "Mother Goodman, I'm Carl Lewis, and this is Lawrence Nelson. You've met us before. We're officers in the Epworth League."

"Oh, yes. Uh...huh. Well, sir, I'll be able to recognize you sooner when my second eyesight comes. You know my...."

"If you'll unlock the door, Mother Goodman," said I, "I'll bring this cider in."

"Spider! Oh, my, we don't want a spider in the house, young man. What's he for — some kind of school museum?"

"You misunderstood. I have some cider, not a spider."

"Oh, I see. Uh...huh. It's not strong, I hope."

"Oh, no ma'am. It's sweet cider, not the kind that makes you drunk."

"I certainly am *not* drunk, young man! I'm just old. I'm 93-year-old. Uh...huh."

"Do you have a lot of children, Mother Goodman?" was Carl's question.

"Well, sir, I have two sons. One is a minister, and the other is a lawyer. I should have...."

"You should have had a doctor son, shouldn't you!" shouted Carl.

By eight o'clock approximately 75 guests were on the lawn, enjoying croquet, washer pitching, table tennis, checkers, dominoes, and talking. The seventy-sixth guest, Professor Holdbolt, who was, of course, still apparently trying to cut his throat on his high collar, was the one person present who seemed to be unhappy. Contributing chiefly to his discomfiture, no doubt, were his persistent checker game defeats at the hands of Brother Goodman.

"My, my, but this is a lovely crowd of young folks, isn't it, Professor Holdbolt?" said the minister as he gave up one man for three of his opponent's.

"You're sure beatin' the Prof bad," Sabor Fang put in. "Want me to help you make your moves, Prof?"

"No, no señor Turner, I'll be all right in a moment. I have these occasional attacks of color blindness, but they usually depart before long, as this one will do presently, and then I'll be able to give Reverend Goodman stiffer competition."

No longer a student of Spanish at the college, Sabor Fang felt himself free to harass the Modern Language head.

"Señor Nelson," he said for the professor's benefit, "speakie you Spanisho?"

"Sí, sí, señor Fang," I responded. "I blabo Spinachy."

A shrill whistle from Bossy Betsy suddenly claimed the crowd's attention.

"Now then, people," she informed, "you are going to form a line here at this table for refreshments. As soon as you finish your refreshments, you will bring your paper cups and dishes and put them here at my feet."

Hurrying to grab a foremost place in line, Bernard Snerd barely smothered a burp as he greeted: "Evening, Brother Goodman!"

"Why, hello there, Bernard!" returned the clergyman, gesturing a salutation and upsetting the checker board. "Professor, that's such a fine young man."

"I'm sorry you disarranged our men, Reverend Goodman. I think my color blindness was disappearing, and I think I would have been the winner from here on out."

When we Beebuzzards had enjoyed several refills in the serving line, we approached Betsy with our paper containers.

"Put them right here at my feet," she commanded stonily.

"Yes, your Royal Highness," said I, and Sharkey, going a bit further, fell upon his knees and bowed low, and then, lifting his hands as if in supplication, he besought, "Take these, oh sovereign queen of the universe, and remember that I didst give my most cherished possessions to thee."

"Begone, knave!" said I. "Canst thou not see that Her Majesty grows weary of thy presence, now that thou hast added thy life's saving to her riches?"

Snickers from the onlookers, a tinge of red in Bossy's cheeks, and an applause from the cottonwood leaves clapping together in the light breeze.

A whistle later, Her Majesty addressed her subjects: "Now if you're not through eating and drinking, you'll just have to quit, because we're going to play a game. I want you to catch hands and form a big circle, and then I want you to number by ones and twos.

The crowd numbered, the leader spoke again: "Each number one will now get behind the person to his or her right. Now then I'm going to start the game by walking around this big circle and putting Brother Goodman's belt in somebody's hand. That person will try to whip me with the belt — until I go all the way around the circle and come back to take my place in front of the whipper's former partner. Then the person holding the belt hands it to somebody and then he runs to safety. By the way, this game is called `smoking hams'. Maybe you can guess why. Now I'm going to start the game by placing the belt in...now let me see...I think — right here!"

Having selected for her pursuer a junior high school lad who was handicapped by weight and short legs, Professor Holdbolt's secretary would easily have stayed out of his belting range but for her tripping over a foot that somehow had extended out too far from the human corral.

"Boy," cackled Sharkey as he massaged his ankle and watched the leather lashing, "she's fairly getting her ham smoked, cured, and sliced, isn't she!"

"Miss Snerd," I called when she had finally reached her place of refuge, "that little stimulation ought to be better than Dr. Hogue's X-ray treatments."

"Lawrence Nelson, you're going too far with your tongue one of these days!"

There were those who fain would withdraw to let their hams cool, but Bossy Besty, as if testing her ability to dominate, compelled them to remain at their posts. Finally when she herself had lost interest in the game, she blew her whistle and announced, "Okay, you may have five minutes to rest and talk, and then we're going to have a big tug of war."

During the intermission, Sabor Fang, knowing that Sharkey was taking a course in abnormal psychology and had been doing some experiments in hypnosis, suggested that he hypnotize someone.

Ignoring the wishes of four others who wanted to be the second party in this experiment, attention-hungry Betsy decreed that she would be Sharkey's subject. To a nearby acquaintance she whispered, "Watch me make a silly monkey out of him."

"Now I've got to have your complete cooperation," the amateur hypnotist told her, as she relaxed in a folding chair opposite him. "Now that you have become thoroughly comfortable, I want you to imagine that you have sat down to rest on the warm bank of a quiet lake. You are tired, and as the rays of a summer sun warm your body you become drowsy...drowsy...sleepy...sleepy...you want to sleep, to rest, for your eyelids are heavy and you want to close them. They are heavy, leaden. You are about to close them."

A hushed silence pervaded the audience throughout the proceedings as Carl continued to make his suggestions of approaching slumber.

"Betsy Snerd," he said at last, "your eyes are fully shut and you are now asleep. You will, however, hear me and obey my instructions. But you will not be aware of anyone else. In fact, there is no one here — only you and I."

To the onlookers he said, "Does someone have an idea about what we ought to have her do?"

"Make her root up a peg," someone suggested. Sabor Fang would have her "shampoo her hair with the rest of that apple cider."

Amid other suggestions came a question: "Can jest anybody hypnotize another person?"

"I should say not!" was Fang's assurance. "It takes somebody with plenty of personality and intelligence...somebody with a sort of magnetism — somebody like Sharkey."

"Gee, I wish I had what it takes to do that," a feminine bystander voiced.

Traces of pride were unavoidably and naturally waltzing in Sharkey's lobes when Betsy suddenly opened hers and said in impatient humor: "I wish you people would hurry and tell him what I'm to do. I'm tired of waiting."

"Well, one can't hypnotize the mentally deficient," abashed Carl said when the circle of laughter had subsided.

Among the few who did not laugh was Harry McDonald, who was resting in a chair on the porch. Nor did he respond to Betsy's command to the group: "Number ones go down to the southern end of the lawn and twos go to the northern."

"Lefty," said Sharkey, "my trouble was wasted on Bossy but not on Major Hoople. That guy's hypnotized. Come on, guy, I've got an idea that's going to give us the last laugh at Bossy's expense."

Since three or four others were beginning to notice Harry's condition, my buddy acted quickly by whispering some instruction in his ear and then snapping him into consciousness with a count of three.

"What did you tell him?" I asked as we left the dairy hand rubbing his eyes and wondering about himself.

"You'll find out just as soon as the screamer on Prof's car pops loose. That's his cue to get the lead out."

The "screamer," as we called it for lack of a better name, was a little explosive cylinder we had bought at a novelty shop especially for attachment to a plug on Professor Holdbolt's immaculate Buick. Grounded to the motor, the diabolical contrivance was waiting for a touch on the starter when it would harmlessly explode, scream and smoke its victim into believing that his automobile was going up in flames.

The tug of war was over and I was regretting that we hadn't thought about clandestinely half severing the rope's middle before the mixer began when I saw he of the swinging neck approach the minister.

"I'm afraid those young people damaged my grass with that last struggle," grumbled the latter, beating the former in a draw of lips. "I certainly hope I won't have to do any replanting. Seeds cost money, you know. But maybe I can get the stewards to buy them."

"Reverend Goodman, I've had a most enjoyable evening, in spite of the checker loss, and I dislike having to leave, but I'm afraid my watch is calling me bedward."

To enjoy the show to follow, we Beebuzzards took ringside seats near the street and the Buick.

"Good night, sir!" said the college faculty member to Brother Goodman just before reaching for the starter.

A startling explosion, a hush from the crowd, smoke's pouring from a whining hood, Prof's frantic scramble to get out, and his appeal. "Quick, young gentlemen, my automobile's on fire! Some water, please! Quick! Hurry, young men, I think my policy has expired."

And then amid the cries and the rush of legs, a scream arose from Bossy Betsy.

"Help!" she appealed as she rolled on the ground with Harry McDonald; he had heard his cue and had gotten the lead out. "He's gone crazy! I'm being attack!"

"So you said you can rassle better'n me!" grunted Harry. "I can push a heifer over with one hand, and...." Here he managed to pin his "opponent's" left shoulder to the ground and simultaneously secure a toe hold.

"Somebody call the Fire Department!" someone suggested, watching the smoking Buick.

"Where's the hose?" someone asked. "Get the hood up quick!"

"Stop it, Harry, you're breaking my foot! Pull him off? He's hurtin' me, I tell you!"

"Hurry, young gentlemen, don't you see my car's on fire!"

But our sole contribution to matters was an occasional "Conflagration! Succor!"

"Call the Fire Department, Marjorie!" This from the pastor to his spouse.

Bernard to his sister's rescue, Bernard on the ground nursing his nose, Bernard moaning.

"Somebody stop him! He's killin' me!"

"Surrender, Betsy? Say `down' an' I'll let you up!"

"Don't get too close to that car, boys!" warned Mrs. Goodman. "There might be an explosion."

"You say there's been a collision?" inquired Mother Goodman, coming from within to ascertain the reason for the outside commotion. "Anybody hurt?"

Another scream from Betsy followed by "Down! Down! I surrender!"

"I think my policy's lapsed."

"Too bad there was a collision, uh...huh."

"Let me have that bucket right here. I'll put it out. Yep, yep. I always did figger I could count on you fellers."

"You oughta known I could lick you. Look at that muscle. I can push a heifer over with that."

CHAPTER TWENTY-SIX

The Gullible Widow

From the living room of my house, Carl and I watched an October rain trying vainly to fill the adobe cracks in the pear orchard ground.

Near the door, my little sister was playing with her dolls, in the kitchen my mother was baking pies, and in the cow barn my father was, yes, pitching manure, as usual.

Suddenly a vagabond vein of mercury in the sky stubbed its toe on a dusky cloud and a moment later cried out in a voice of thunder.

"You hear that, bubber?" said Helen. "Bet that's somebody shootin' firecrackers in heaven. Huh?"

"Ask Carl, little sis. He can tell you all about it."

"Honey, suppose I just tell you a story instead?"

"Okay, but not 'bout the horse on top of the hill. I don't like those kind of words."

"Then I'll tell you about a mule that lived on top of the hill."

"No, no, I don't want you tell me 'bout the hill!"

"All right, honey. I'll tell you about a man that had a whole yard full of pets. He had a hen, a horse, a dog, a cow, a goat, and a rabbit. One day the man decided he would move many miles away. But how would he take all his animal friends in the one little cart he had? At last the horse said, `Master, I know how you can do it. You can put Mrs. Chicken in first....'"

"Was that the selfish ol' chicken that drank all the horse's water?"

"No, this was another one."

"Carl, did you know we gonna have chicken for dinner?"

"My, my," was Carl's impersonation of Brother Goodman, "but I'm fond of fried chicken! I was just telling Marjorie last week there's nothing I like better than fried chicken."

"Carl, you ever twist a chicken's neck an' shell him?"

"She means, did you ever wring one's neck and pick its feathers," I interpreted.

"Tell me some more story, Carl."

"Well, the horse told the farmer that he could first put the chicken in the cart, then put the rabbit on her back, the dog on his, the cow on the dog's back, and the horse on the cow's back."

"But he can't do that!" protested the alarmed child. "Thas not the way. He gotta put the big people on the bottom so they won't slop over and get all smashed on the ground!"

Powdered with flour, my mother left her pastries long enough to learn the cause of her daughter's sobs and to request, "Please, Carl, for goodness sakes, reverse the order the those b-e-a-s-t-s!"

The hen was clucking from a rodent balcony and the horse was neighing on the basement layer when Helen remembered that the goat was not on board.

"Why the man don't take the goat? He gonna leave the goat 'cause he don't like him 'cause he got whiskers an' he don't shave like daddy do? Huh?"

The dove of peace was quick to coo its approval when the narrator quickly inserted the goat between the dog and the horse.

Helen had hardly left us to sample pie filling when I turned to my buddy and inquired: "Lad, do you know a Mrs. Alton Morris, a pretentious and gossipy widow who lives on Pierce Drive?"

"The bridge fiend, that thin wren who could stand all day in the Sahara without casting a shadow?"

"The same. And you might also add the woman who believes in seances and otherwise falls hook, line, and sinker for almost any kind of quackery that comes her way."

"And why does she trespass upon your thoughts, my wistful wit?"

"Methinks, Sir Carl, the dame spendeth too much time on said cards to the neglect of other matters. Methinks it's our Christian duty to administer a bit of chastisement. Whilst thou was speaking lies to the child a few burps back, I did make plans for the dame. Let us eject our lead and retire to the telephone in yon bedroom."

I was "Lord McKinny, a bridge expert from Liverpool, England," I told the gullible one.

"Of course you've heard of me, have you not, Mrs. Morris?"

"Oh, er, why, yes, Lord McKinney."

"Well, Mrs. Morris, I'm heah in your little hamlet for a short sojourn between busses, and, upon learning that you are a prominent figure in one of Mesa's leading cawd clubs, I said to my Personality A, 'McKinney, ol' fellow, you should jolly well enjoy a bridge conference with this Mrs. Morris, wouldn't you now?'"

"Well, Lord McKinney" was the answer at the other end, "I'd jest be real pro...I mean simply delighted to have you."

"Oh, but my deah, first I must finish telling you about this conversation between my dual personalities. Well, when my Personality A awsked my Personality B if he would enjoy a conference with you, I was frightfully astonished at the reply the beastly chap made. He's quite a rascal, I'm afraid, but an entertaining sort sometimes, if I may say so. Know wot he said, my deah Mrs. Morris?"

"Oh, then you're a student of the psychic, Lord McKinney! Ain'...I mean isn't that wunderful! And what did your Personality B have to say? I jest know this sure is going to be ever so intriguing!"

"Well, the unpredictable reprobate said, 'Wot, subject yourself to an hour of beastly boredom in this poor wenche's hovel just to chatter about cawds?' And then he..."

"Well! He...he cer...."

"Oh, but deah Mrs. Morris, you should have heard the scolding my Personality A gave the ruffian! Said he, 'Why, you uncouth rogue, Mrs. Morris may be a miserable wench to you, but I'm sure I shall find her a gracious lady of charm, culture, and refinement.' So you see, Mrs. Morris, I have two reasons for wanting to meet you: to exchange a few bridge plays with you and to prove Personality B is a perfect cad."

"Why, I'll jest be tic...I mean delighted to have you! When will you come?"

"Well, Mrs. Morris, I think I can spare you an hour tonight between eight and nine."

"Good! I'll sure be expecting you then and looking forward to making...I mean meeting you, Lord Mc...."

"Now you will realize, of course, Mrs. Morris, that I'm a rather busy fellow and have other engagements, so you will please have the playing table and chairs set up and everything in perfect readiness at eight. Do I make myself quite clear, Mrs. Morris?"

"Oh, yes, indeed!"

"One otha thing, Mrs. Morris. I will simply not partake of alcoholic liquors for refreshment. I am a man of simple tastes and very easily pleased. A plain mint julep without the brandy and the mint will suffice my requirements."

"But how...."

"How do you prepare mint julep without the mint and the brandy? Confound it, woman, why make a stupid ass of yourself! Use your mind! You have one, I hope. Or do you?"

"My deah Mrs. Morris," I purred, after my tempestuous outburst, "that was Personality B who spoke so offensively. Please be assured that Personality A will reprove him quite soundly for his nasty behavior, and be further assured that before coming to your home tonight we shall try to have his solemn pledge to remain in the background throughout the evening. I do hope the fellow won't try to take over. Sometimes he is quite a jokester, and sometimes quite amusing, I dare say."

And now it became Sharkey's turn to telephone, for he was our Brother Goodman impersonator. The supplementary part in the project in progress required, I explained to my fellow Beebuzzard, that Foxy Mack be instructed to call at the home of our victim at eight to identify himself and tell her he had come for her card table for a parsonage lawn party.

A few minutes after eight we were screened securely behind a tumble weed when Foxy knocked at the semi-rural home on Pierce Drive.

"Yes? Who is it?" the widow called from within.

"It's me — Loyd McKinney."

The door swung slowly open, and Mrs. Morris said to the dark form, "You'll excuse my caution, Lord McKinney, but they've...I mean, there've been prowlers about, and a girl all by her lonesome has to be careful, you know. You do...."

The light from within revealed the long nose of Mr. McKinney and his jacketed blue denims.

"Is the card table ready, Mrs. Morris?"

Silence and then a bewildered: "You...but I thought you said you...oh, I thought you said you were Lord McKinney. I guess I was just think...."

"But I am Loyd McKinney, lady. Yep, yep, been that way all my life."

"Then you...oh, I get it. How foolish of me! Why, it's Personality B tryin' a trick on me. For a minute I thought you was someone else."

"No, ma'am, it's jest Loyd McKinney."

"You told me what a jokester he was. I should have known right away. I can see right now we're sure going to have an interesting evening together.

"Lady, I'm a married man and you're a widow woman. I can't spend th' night with you."

"Well, I certainly didn't ask you to spend the night with me, Lord McKinney. But you...."

"You got the table ready?"

"Yes, come on in and...are you sure...Lord McKinney, I sure wish you'd get rid of this personality."

"Lady, I'm too old to start changin'. I don't need no personality for my job, anyways."

"I don't see why you put up with it." A deep sigh. "Well, now you jest come on in and have that drink I fixed and maybe you'll...."

"I ain't no drinker, Mrs. Morris. All I want is that table."

"But we've got a lot of time for that, Lord McKinney."

"I tell you I got a wife. What would people say? Yep, yep, might lose my job an' wife too! Gimme that table now!"

For a moment, vaporous clouds hiding the rocky face of Old Rusty in the east made like a great photo shutter, letting in a gigantic eye of moonlight. Then lowering a quick concealing fog, it seemed to create a chiding wink, which we two pranking Beebuzzards felt was meant for us.

CHAPTER TWENTY-SEVEN

We Shall Return, Mesa!

Like Arabian stallions galloping across the sand dunes, the years raced all too quickly over the plains of time and matter, separating the Beebuzzards and dashing them into drab conventionality.

And yet Carl, with his wife Eleanor, and I, with my Esterlene would not exchange the present for the past. For now, thanks to the practical influences of our spouses, we have become acceptable and normal members of society...and we are happy. And we can still laugh just as heartily as we did the time we sewed up the panel in Harry McDonald's flannels and fed him a series of laxative Feenamints, which he assumed was regular chewing gum.

Carl and I have not haunted Mesa with our presense for a number of years. But the gentle populace must not assume that we shall not return, for we still have one bit of business to attend to — one last fling at Beebuzzardism, one final prank to play to bring the downy ones to roost.

That old bell hanging silent and unknown in the unapparent church belfry — we're still going to ring it and at a time we agreed upon years ago.

Not quite so agile as we were in the yesteryears when we played hide-and-go-seek with Mesa's deputy summoned to investigate strange noises and songs in the old building's basement, this time we shall probably be apprehended.

And if this novel becomes a souvenir hunter of rejection slips, someone will doubtless put us on a bean diet or send us away to some quiet rest home. On the other hand, if it gains recognition as a seller, I shall flash an indentification card in my pocketbook and accept his friendly handshake.

Moreover, should this yarn pull the wool over the public's eyes enough to fetch me the price of a root beer, I shall be obliged to give a banquet in honor of the characters we made unhappy in the thing sometimes — seemingly.

Last night I dropped into dreamland and fancied that I had really gathered these people together for this occasion.

"Ladies and gentlemen," I said, looking past Filbert's bright Meskin shirt and Professor Holdbolt's white strangler, "touched by an overwhelming spirit of generosity, I feel moved at this time to give to each of you my very best autograph!"

"Incidentally," I added, "you will find the autograph at the bottom of a check for 300 dollars each."

"I always knew I could count on at least one of you fellers," mumbled he of the racing snout.

"Don't do it, son," Cousin Boyd protested. "Save your money. You're liable to need it when somebody here sues you for some things you said about 'em."

"Somebody pick Cousin Boyd up off the floor" was my request seconds later. "What happened to your teeth, Cousin Boyd? Don't tell me the chicken was that tough! And what in the world happened to your knuckles, Brother Goodman? Why they're bleeding!"

As I pen these concluding lines, I can't ignore the ringing advice my cousin gave me in that dream. Moreover, another thought has occurred to me: Would not such a gathering be photographed and the faces of these people paraded on the news front?

Here at the very end, I have definitely decided against the mass banquet. The advice I shall heed came from Carl soon after I had come upon him as he was scolding one of his high school freshmen: "Why as a boy, Stanley, I never would have thought of doing such a mischievous thing!"

Carl's suggestion was this: "Guy, let's make the feed simple and just have it down at your cafe, just for the three of us — you, me, and Jasper O. Rice."

The End